Correction, Instruction

A Treatise of Afflictions

Thomas Case

Soli Deo Gloria Publications
An imprint of Reformation Heritage Books
Grand Rapids, Michigan

Soli Deo Gloria Publications
An imprint of Reformation Heritage Books
3070 29th St. SE
Grand Rapids, MI 49512
616-977-0889
orders@heritagebooks.org
www.heritagebooks.org

This facsimile is taken from *Correction, Instruction; or, A Treatise of Afflictions* (London: Religious Tract Society, 1836).

Paperback edition published 2025

ISBN 979-8-88686-212-6

Printed in the United States of America
25 26 27 28 29 30/10 9 8 7 6 5 4 3 2 1

CONTENTS

Address to the Author 3

Extract from Epistle to the Reader (1671) 5

To the Reader 11

Text 13

> "Blessed is the man whom thou chastenest, O LORD,
> and teachest him out of thy law." —Psalm 94:12

Doctrine 14

> That man is a blessed man whose chastisements
> are joined with divine teachings.

Particulars

    I. Lessons God Teaches His People by Chastisements . 15

    II. The Nature and Properties of Divine Teaching 87

    III. How Correction Tends Toward Instruction 105

    IV. Grounds and Demonstrations of the Point 110

Uses 116

    Information 117

    Exhortation 136

CORRECTION, INSTRUCTION;

or

A TREATISE OF AFFLICTIONS

FIRST CONCEIVED

BY WAY OF PRIVATE MEDITATIONS;

AFTERWARD

DIGESTED INTO CERTAIN SERMONS, AND NOW PUBLISHED FOR THE HELP AND COMFORT OF HUMBLE SUFFERING CHRISTIANS.

BY THOMAS CASE, M.A.

SOMETIME STUDENT OF CHRIST CHURCH, OXFORD. PREACHER OF THE GOSPEL IN LONDON, A.D. 1652

Though He slay me, yet will I trust in Him, **Job 13:15**

SIR,

I THANK you for the favour you did me in affording me a sight of your papers; I had heard much of your notions concerning afflictions, and therefore was very thirsty till you were pleased to give me to drink of the fountain: I can now say as that queen, "The half was not told me," 1 Kings x. 7. fame came much short of taste: we are perfect in no lessons so much as those into which God whippeth us; and cannot speak of any argument so warmly and feelingly, as when we speak out of present experience. To treat of afflictions when we ourselves flourish and abound in ease and plenty, savoureth more of the orator than the preacher, the brain than the heart: certainly guess and imagination cannot so well introduce such conceptions as sense and feeling.

It seemeth when you went into prison the Spirit of God went into prison with you; and when you were shut up to others, you still lay open to the visits and free breathings of his grace: the restraints and enclosures of a prison cannot prejudice the freedom of his operations. He is a close prisoner indeed that is shut up not only from the society of men, but converse with the Holy Ghost. I begin to see there is somewhat more than a strain and reach of wit in Tertullian's consolatory discourse to the Martyrs : " You went out of prison," saith he, " when you went into it, and were but sequestered from the world, that you might converse with God ; the greatest prisoners and the most guilty are those that are at large, darkened with ignorance, chained with lusts, committed not by the proconsul, bu‍: God," &c. The Lord often manifested himself to his prophets in a wilderness, and to you in you, secession and retirement.

Sir, I could even envy your prison comforts, and the sweet opportunities of a religious privacy. We that are abroad are harassed and worn out with constant public labours, and can seldom retire from the distraction of business for such free converse with God and our own souls : but we are not to choose our own portion ; crosses will come soon enough without wishing for them ; and if we were wise we might make an advantage of every condition.

Good sir, be persuaded to publish those discourses ; the subject is useful, and your manner of handling it warm and affectionate ; do not deprive the world of the comfort of your experiences. Certainly my heart is none of the tenderest ; yet if heart answereth heart, I can easily foresee much success, and that you will not repent of the publication. The Lord bless your endeavours in the gospel of his dear Son.

I am, sir,

Yours in all christian observance,

THOMAS MANTON.

EXTRACT

FROM THE

EPISTLE TO THE READER.

PUBLISHED WITH THE SECOND EDITION.

A. D. 1671.

READER,—This brief discourse before thee is an epistle in itself, not mine but God's, containing matter of counsel and comfort, to the generation of his sufferers. It was written not many years ago, and yet it wanteth a new impression, the chief account whereof may be that which the apostle giveth in a like case, "You have forgotten the exhortation which speaketh unto you as unto children," &c. Heb. xii. 5. Truly there is the reason of all our non-proficiency under Divine teaching. We forget the doctrine before we come to the use: by means whereof, we are as great strangers to the cross, when we come to suffer, as if we had never heard of it; and thereby it cometh to pass that we do either despise the chastisement of the Lord, or else faint when we are rebuked of him. If the affliction be in measure, as the scripture phrase is, Isa. xxvii. 3. we are apt to despise it, as not worth taking notice of: but if the rod fetch blood, presently it is intolerable, and we begin to faint, crying out in our passion, Was ever sorrow like my sorrow? as if we could have borne any burden but that upon the back.

It is very sad to observe, suffering, persecution especially, hath got an ill name in the world. The devil and a reprobate world have brought up a scandal upon the cross, whilst sufferings immediately from God are interpreted as the fruits and evidences of God's hatred; to obviate which discouragement the apostle spends the twelve first verses of Heb. xii. by many irrefragable arguments, the main whereof is the instance of all instances, the unparalleled sufferings of the Son of God, to establish this conclusion, as a cordial to keep the hearts of all the suffering saints of God from fainting; namely, that God's rod and God's love may stand together.

Sufferings likewise from men, persecution, as for the gospel's sake, are accounted no better than the stigmata of malefactors, marks of sedition and rebellion against civil government: upon which the ignorant malicious multitude begin to cry out against them, as the heathen of old, Away with these christians, cast them into the lion's den;

Providence having so ordered it, that whosoever with Caleb, will follow the Lord fully, Num. xiv. 24. shall be exposed to the world's hatred; and not their persons only but their sufferings, be laden with the basest obloquies that the wit of malice can invent. They are reputed as:

The troublers of Israel,

The pests of human societies,

Persons not fit to live in the world, &c.

And verily the world speak as truly of them as they speak vilely; their censures did not exceed the bounds of justice; but the *cause* makes the martyr, not the *punishment.*

This duty considered, it is, not less than to wonder, observable with what titles of honour the Spirit of God in holy scriptures is pleased to dignify the sufferings of the saints, when, I say, they suffer, as christians, that is to say—

For righteousness' sake, Matt. v. 10. 1 Pet. iii. 14.

For the name of Christ, 1 Pet. iv. 14.

Not because they have sinned, but because they will not sin, Psa. xliv. 22. 1 Pet. iv. 4, 5.

When for the kingdom of God, 2 Thess. i. 5.

When they suffer that the truth of the gospel may not suffer, Gal. ii. 5.

In these cases and the like, the sufferings of the saints, however they may be ignominiously traduced, 1 Pet. iv. 14. by men that are not competent judges either of the saints or of the sufferings, 1 Cor. ii. 15.

yet they are most honourably attested by the un-
erring witness of the Holy Ghost; they are called:

Christians' letters testimonial for heaven, Matt.v.10.

The gift of God, Phil. i. 29. Answerable to that
account which our Lord had of his own sufferings,
John xviii. 11. "The cup which my Father hath
given me, shall I not drink it?"

The appearance of the glorious Spirit resting
upon them, 1 Pet. iv. 14.

Their baptism for, and consecration to their
heavenly inheritance, Mark x. 38, 39.

The after sufferings of Jesus Christ, without
which Christ's sufferings, as a body, are not com-
plete; though, as a Mediator, they were perfect
upon the cross at what time he cried out, "It is
finished."

Their evangelical perfection, James i. 4; and no
wonder, for sufferings were Christ's perfection, Heb.
ii. 10.

A refining pot for their faith, 1 Pet. i. 7.

The improvement of their graces, 1 Pet. i. 6, 7.

The enhancement of their glory, 2 Cor. iv. 17.

Their conformity to Christ their Head, 2 Tim. ii.
11, 12.

In a word, glorious things are spoken of sufferers
and their sufferings, for the testimony of Jesus.

For the reviving whereof upon the heads and
hearts of all Christ's confessors and martyrs, it hath
been earnestly begged by some that wish well to

the interest of the gospel, that these prison notions might be reprinted.

The Lord give them, indeed, a new impression, that they may be known to be "the epistle of Christ ministered by us, written not with ink, but with the Spirit of the living God; not in tables of stone, but in fleshy tables of the heart," 2 Cor. iii. 3.

Surely discourses of affliction can never be unseasonable. The scripture tells us, that "many are the sufferings of the righteous," Psa. xxxiv. 19; and daily experience verifieth it: God chasteneth them, because they are no better, the devil and the reprobate world hate them, because they are so good. The evil spirit stirreth up his instruments to vex and molest the saints, that he may make an advantage of their troubles, one way or other, to hinder the course of the gospel. Most of his assaults are conveyed to us by afflictions: therefore when we are bidden to resist the devil, stedfast in the faith, we are told immediately, that the "same afflictions are accomplished in our brethren that are in the world," 1 Pet. v. 9.

Possibly an hour of temptation may be nearer to us than we are willing to believe.

Let us not begin to flatter ourselves with the vain confidence that God will not punish his people by those that are worse than themselves, Hab. i. 13. England hath sinned at that rate, that God may justify himself in the severe execution of that bitter reproach once threatened against a people, altogether as good as ourselves; " I will bring the worst of the heathen, and they shall possess your houses," Ezek. vii. 24.

For the preventing of so shameful a destruction, (if yet by Divine prerogative it may be prevented,) let us take the course of God's own prescribing, by sound repentance and solemn reconciliation, to prepare to meet our God, and lay hold of his strength that we make peace with him, Isa. xxvii. 5. Let us do this; and then, if judgment come, judgment itself can do us no harm: but otherwise, if mercy come, even mercy itself can do us no good. The Lord teach us, in this our day, to know the things of our peace, before they be hid from our eyes.

TO THE READER.

Reader, thou hast here in these following leaves some prison-thoughts—I wish I could say experiences. If I have not written herein what I have found, I bless God, I have written what I have sought. I must humbly confess with holy Paul, "I count not myself to have apprehended;" yet through grace I can add with that blessed saint, "but this one thing I do, forgetting those things which are behind, and reaching forth unto those things which are before, I press towards the mark," Phil. iii. 13, 14. God hath taught me somewhat of the doctrine, if he would please to teach me the use; God hath in some measure showed me what is to be gained by afflictions, if he would also teach me how to gain it, I should with Moses, account my sufferings "greater riches than the treasures of Egypt," Heb. xi. 26. The discovery is sweet; if my heart deceive me not, I would not exchange it for the wealth of both the Indies; the possession infinitely precious. For thy advantage I have been persuaded to print. My prayers shall accompany my papers, that that God, who quickeneth the dead, and calleth things that are not as though they were, would please to make these broken expressions answer the aim; and for the aim's sake despise them not, but pray thou also: and when thou prayest, remember the chiefest of sinners, the poor and unworthy author, who, whilst yet in the land of the living, will be thine, to serve thee, in the gospel of Christ,

THOMAS CASE.

CORRECTION, INSTRUCTION.

THE ROD AND THE WORD.

PSALM XCIV. 12.

BLESSED IS THE MAN WHOM THOU CHASTENEST, O LORD,
AND TEACHEST HIM OUT OF THY LAW.

THIS psalm being without a title, it is not so easily determined when, or by whom it was penned: probably by David, when himself, and the rest of the godly party, were under a sore and bitter persecution by Saul, and others of that bloody and hypocritical faction that bare sway under him.

Briefly, in the psalm the prophet doth these three things.

First. He doth appeal to God for vengeance on the persecutors; describing them by their pride, ver. 2. profaneness, ver. 3, 4. their intemperate virulency of speech, ver. 4. cruelty and bloody practices, ver. 5, 6. and, lastly, by their atheistical security, ver. 7.

Second. He turns to address the enemies, endeavouring to convince them of the brutishness and folly of their atheism, the mother and nurse of the other impieties charged on them, ver. 8. and that by a threefold argument.

1. The power and skill of God in creating the hearing and seeing organ in man, ver. 9.

B

2. The sovereignty of God, and the righteousness of his judgments, which he executes in the world, ver. 10. the former part.

3. His wisdom and knowledge, in enduing man with such an excellent intellectual faculty, whereby even the creature itself is able to attain to admirable degrees of knowledge, ver. 10, 11.

4. He labours to comfort the godly against all the pressures and persecutions under which they did groan and languish.

The first argument which the psalmist useth to this purpose is in the text, namely, the sweet fruit which is to be gathered from the bitter root of affliction; the root indeed is bitter but the fruit is sweet, even Divine instruction, which therefore is no longer to be esteemed a punishment, but a blessing.

"Blessed is the man whom thou chastenest, O Lord, and teachest him out of thy law."

This being the subject I intend to insist upon, I shall without any more ado contract it into this doctrinal point of observation.

> THAT MAN IS A BLESSED MAN, WHOSE CHAS-
> TISEMENTS ARE JOINED WITH DIVINE TEACH-
> INGS ; OR,
>
> IT IS A BLESSED THING WHEN CORRECTION AND
> INSTRUCTION GO TOGETHER. THE ROD AND
> THE WORD MAKE UP A COMPLETE BLESSING.

I shall take chastisements here in the utmost latitude, for all kinds and degrees of sufferings, whether from God, or man, or Satan; whether sufferings for sin, or sufferings for righteousness' sake. And for the doctrinal part of the point, I shall endeavour these four things.

I. To show you what those lessons are which God doth teach his people by his chastisements.

II. What the nature and properties of Divine teachings are.

III. In what tendency correction lieth in order unto these teachings; or, what use God doth make of affliction for the carrying on of the work of instruction in the hearts of his people.

IV. I shall lay down the grounds and demonstrations of the point; or, considerations to evince the happiness of that man whom God is pleased to teach by his corrections.

I begin with the lessons which God doth usually teach his people in a suffering condition. Amongst many which may fall within the experience of the suffering saints of God, I shall observe unto you twenty several lessons, which when I have presented at large, I shall then contract into three summary and comprehensive instructions, which will contain the substance of all.

1. The first lesson which God teacheth by affliction, is, compassion towards them which are in a suffering condition. Truly we are very prone to be insensible of our brethren's sufferings, when we ourselves are at ease in Zion: partly by reason of that sensuality which is in our natures, reigning in carnal men, and dwelling even in the regenerate themselves, whereby we let out our hearts so inordinately to the creature comforts which we possess, as to quench the tenderness and sense which we ought to have of the miseries and hardships of other men: partly out of the delicacy of self-love, which makes us unwilling to sour the relish of our own sweet fruitions with the bitter taste of strangers' afflictions: partly through sluggishness and torpor of spirit, which makes us unwilling to rise up from the bed of ease and pleasure to travail in the

inquiry of the state of our brethren either abroad or at home; so that, as the apostle saith in another case, we are willingly ignorant, and are not only strangers, but are content to be strangers to their miseries and calamities.

One way or other, even christians themselves, and such as are truly so called, are more or less guilty of the sin of the Gentiles; "without natural affection, unmerciful," Rom. i. 31. without bowels, without compassion.

Hence you may find, that it was one of the errands upon which God sent Israel into Egypt, that in the brick-kilns there their hard hearts might be softened and melted into compassion towards strangers and captives. Therefore when God had turned their captivity, that was one of the first lessons of which he puts them in mind, "Thou shalt not oppress a stranger;" there is the duty, which, though negatively expressed, yet, according to the rule of interpreting the commandments, doth include all the affirmative duties of mercy and compassion; and the motive follows, "for ye know the heart of a stranger." How came they to know it? "seeing ye were strangers in the land of Egypt." As if God had said, I knew thou hadst a heart of iron and bowels of brass within thee, incompassionate and cruel, and therefore, I sent you into Egypt, on purpose that by the cruelty of the Egyptians I might intender your hearts, and that by the experience of your own sufferings and miseries you might learn as long as you live to lay to heart the anguish and agonies of strangers and captives; that whensoever you see a stranger in your habitations, you may say, O here is a poor sojourner, an exile, I will surely have mercy upon him, and show him kindness, for

I myself have been a stranger and a bond-slave in Egypt; I know by experience what a fearful, trembling, bleeding heart he carrieth in his bosom, &c.

And upon this very account God still brings variety of afflictions and sorrows upon his own children; he suffereth them to be plundered, banished, imprisoned, reduced to great extremities, that by their own experience they may learn to draw out their souls to the hungry, and mercies towards such objects of pity; that they might say within themselves, I know the heart of this afflicted soul; I know what it is to be plundered, to be rich one day, and the very next day to be stript naked of all one's comforts and accommodations. I know what it is to hear poor hunger-starved children cry for bread, and there is none to give them. I know what it is to be banished from dearest relations, to be like arms and legs torn out of the body, and to lie bleeding in their separation. I know what it is to be cast into prison, to be locked up alone in the dark, with no other company but one's own fears and sorrows. I know what it is to receive the sentence of death in ourselves, &c. Shall not I pity, and pray, and pour out my soul over such as are bleeding and languishing under the like miseries? And this argument yet makes deeper impression, when a christian compares and measures his lighter burden of affliction with another's more grievous yoke, and reasons thus within himself; Imprisonment was grievous to me, and yet I enjoyed many comforts and accommodations, which others have not; I had a sweet chamber, and a soft bed, when some poor members of Jesus Christ, in the Spanish Inquisition, and the Turkish slavery, are cast into the dungeon, and sink, with Jeremiah, into the mire; their feet are hurt in the stocks, and the irons do enter into their soul; others lie bleeding and gasping upon the cold ground with their undressed wounds, exposed to all the injuries of hunger and nakedness in the open air. I saw the face of my christian friends, sometimes enjoyed refreshment in converse with dearest relations, while some of God's precious people are cast into dark and stinking prisons, and do not see the face of a christian, not of a man possibly in five, ten, or twenty years together, unless it be of their torment-ers. I had fresh diet every day, not only for neces-sity but for delight, while other precious servants of God want their necessary bread, lie starving in the doleful places of their sorrowful restraint, and would be glad to eat the worst of food, even that which would be most loathsome to me. Oh shall not my bowels yearn, and my compassions be rolled within me, towards such objects of misery and compassion?

Truly, brethren, we see it daily in case of the stone, toothache, gout, and the like evils, how ex-perience doth melt the heart into tears of sym-pathy and fellow-feeling, while strangers to such sufferings stand wondering at, and almost deriding the heart-breaking laments of poor wretches. Bre-thren, that you may not wonder at this, consider I beseech you what the apostle speaks of Christ himself; "It behoved him in all things to be made like unto his brethren, that he might be a merciful and faithful High Priest in things pertaining to God," Heb. ii. 17. And again, "We have not a High Priest which cannot be touched with the feeling of our infirmities, but was in all points tempted like as we are, yet without sin," Heb. iv. 15.

A man would say within himself, Why what need had the Lord Jesus to invest himself with a body of flesh that he might know the infirmities of our nature, since he was God, and knew all things? Nay, but, my brethren, it seems the knowledge which Christ had as God, was different from that knowledge which he had as man; that which he had as God, was intuitive; that which he had as man, was experimental : experimental knowledge of misery is the heart-affecting knowledge; and therefore Christ himself would intender his own heart, as Mediator, by his own sense and feeling. And if the Lord Jesus, who was mercy itself, would put himself into a suffering condition, that he might the more sweetly and affectionately act those mercies towards his suffering members, how much more do we, that by nature are incompassionate and cruel, need such practical teachings to work upon our own hearts! Certainly we cannot gain so much sense of the saints' sufferings by the most artificial and skilful relation that the tongue of men or angels is able to express, no nor by all our scripture knowledge, yea though sanctified, as we do by one day's experience in the school of affliction, when God is pleased to be the school-master.

This is one end why God sends us thither, and the first lesson we learn by affliction—sympathy with, and compassion to our suffering brethren.

2. I come to the second lesson, and that is, by chastisements God doth teach us how to prize our outward mercies and comforts more, and yet to dote upon them less; to be more thankful for them, and yet less ensnared by them. This is a mystery

indeed to nature, a paradox to the world; for naturally we are very prone either to slight, or to surfeit. And yet, it is sad to consider, we can make a shift to do both at once; we can undervalue our mercies even while we glut ourselves with them, and despise them even when we are surfeiting upon them. Witness that caution inculcated by Moses and Joshua, " When thou hast eaten and art full, take heed thou forget not the Lord thy God," Deut. viii. 10—12. vi. 11, 12. Behold, while men fill themselves with the mercies of God, they can neglect the God of their mercies. When God is most liberal in remembering us, we are most ungrateful to forget God. Now therefore that we may know how to put a due estimate upon mercies, God often cuts us short, that we may learn to prize that by want, which our foolish unthankful hearts slighted in the enjoyment. Thus the prodigal, who, while yet at home, could despise the rich and well-furnished table of his father, when God sent him to school to the swine-trough, could value the bread tha. the servants did eat; " How many of my father's hired servants have bread enough, and to spare !" Luke xv. 17. He would have been glad of the reversion of broken meat that was cast into the common basket.

I do not believe David ever slighted the ordinances, yet certainly he never knew so well how to estimate them, as when he was banished from them; then a porter's place, the sparrow's nest, and the swallow's neighbourhood to the altar of God, were matters of envy to him, Psa. lxxxiv. The remembrance of the company of saints, the beauty of the ordinances, Psa. xlii. 4. cx. 3. and the presence of God, Psa. lxiii. 2. fetcheth tears from his eyes, and groans from his heart, in his sorrowful exile: "When I remember these things, I pour out my soul in me, &c. My tears are my meat day and night," Psa. xlii. 3, 4. Oh how amiable are the assemblies of the saints, and the ordinances of the sabbath, when we are deprived of them! "In those days the word of the Lord was precious," 1 Sam. iii. 1. *Obj.* When was it not precious? *Ans.* It was always precious in the worth of it: but now it was precious for the want of it: prophets and prophecy were precious because rare; so it followeth, "There was no open vision." Want will teach us the worth of mercies. Our liberties and dearest relations how cheap and common things are they while we possess them without any check or restraint! While we have the keeping of our mercies in our own hands, we make but small reckoning of them. Oh, but let God threaten a divorce by death or banishment, let task-masters be set over us and our comforts, who shall measure out unto us at their own pleasure; let us be locked up awhile under close imprisonment, and there be kept fasting from our dearest enjoyments, then the sight of a friend though but through an iron grate, the exchange of a few common civilities with a yoke-fellow under the correction and control of a keeper, how sweet and precious! Whereas months and years of arbitrary enjoyments are past through, and we scarcely sit down to reflect one serious view upon our mercies; seldom spread them before the Lord in prayer, or send up one thankful ejaculation to God by night upon our beds, in this or the like manner; Lord, what mercy is this which I enjoy in my yoke-fellow, children, friends, liberty, estate, comforts, and accommodations of all sorts, not for necessity only, but for delight, while others, better than I, languish under an unequal yoke, have great rebukes in their children, are separated from friends, despoiled of their estates, imprisoned, banished, afflicted, deserted, tormented! How comes it to pass that so much mercy falls to my share? that I want nothing, while others have nothing? &c. Oh how rarely do we entertain such discourses with our own hearts, but pass by mercies as common things, scarcely worth the owning, whereas in the house of bondage, in a land of captivity, the lees and dregs of those mercies will be precious, which while the vessel ran full and fresh we could hardly relish. In famine the very gleanings of our comforts are better than the whole vintage in the years of plenty.

And then also, as God teacheth us to prize our mercies, so by affliction also he doth teach us moderation in the use of them; while we value, not to surfeit. And indeed it is the inordinate use of outward comforts which renders us unfit to prize them; we lose our esteem of mercies in excess. Surfeits do usually render those things nauseous, which formerly have been our delicacies. By our excesses in creature enjoyments, reason is drowned in sense, judgment extinguished in appetite, and the affections being blunted by commonness of exercise, even pleasures themselves become a burden. Surely the excessive letting out of ourselves to sensual fruitions, is both a sin and a punishment, while thereby we lose both the creature, and God, and ourselves at once.

Now this distemper God doth many times cure by the sharp corrosive of affliction, and by hardship teacheth us moderation: partly by inuring us to abatements and wants, whereby that which at first was necessity, afterwards grows to be our choice. Hence saith the apostle, " I have learned to want," Phil. iv. 12. How? why God had taught him to live on a little. By feeding us sparingly, God abates and slackens the inordinacy of the appetite. Partly and especially, God takes off our hearts from inordinate indulgences in a suffering condition, by discovering richer and purer satisfactions in Jesus Christ. It is God's design by withdrawing the creature, to invite, and fix the soul upon himself. The voice of the rod is, O taste, and see how good the Lord is! which when the soul hath once perceived, thrusting the creature away with contempt and indignation, it opens itself to God, saying, " Whom have I in heaven but thee? and there is none upon earth that I desire in comparison of thee," Psa. lxxiii. 25. Surely it was in the school of affliction that David learned that lesson, even when the wicked prospered, and himself, with the rest of the godly, were plagued all the day long, and chastened every morning, Psa. lxxiii. 14.

This is the second, and a happy lesson, to prize comforts more, and yet dote upon our comforts less.

3. A third lesson, which God teacheth by his chastisements, is, self-denial and obediential submission to the will of God.

In our prosperity we are full of our own wills, and usually we give God counsel when God looks for obedience, as if we could tell God how it might have been better; and so we dispute our cross when we should take it up; but now by bearing a little we learn to bear more; the trial of our faith worketh patience: the more we suffer, the more God fits us for suffering, James i. 3. partly by working us off from our own wills: folly is bound up in the heart of God's children, as well as our own ; "but the rod of correction driveth it far from them," Prov. xxii. 15. God fetcheth out the stubbornness and perverseness of our spirits by the discipline of the rod. So that before he hath done with us, we have not a will to lift up against his will. And surely as we say to our children, Oh, it is a good rod, which breaks us of our obstinacy. Partly by inuring us to the cross. The bullock unaccustomed to the yoke, is very impatient under the hand of the husbandman ; but after he is inured to labour, he willingly puts his neck under the yoke: and so it is with christians, after a while the yoke of affliction begins to be well settled, and by much bearing we learn to bear with quietness. A new cart maketh a great noise and squeaking, but when once used, it goeth silently under the greatest load. None murmur so much at sufferings as they who have suffered least: whereas on the contrary, we see many times that they are most patient who have the heaviest burden upon their backs. "He sitteth alone, and keepeth silence, because he hath borne it upon him," Lam. iii. 28. which means, he is patient because he is acquainted with sorrows. When people cry out, "Oh, never such sufferings as mine," it is an argument they are strangers to afflictions. Partly also because by chastisements God works out by degrees the delicacy of spirit which we contract in our prosperity ; mercy makes us tender. They who are always kept in the warm house, dare not put their head out of doors in a storm: none so unfit for sufferings as they that have been always dandled upon the knee of Pro-vidence: the most delicate constitutions are most unfit for hardship. But lastly and chiefly, this comes to pass because by suffering we come to taste the fruit of sufferings. "No chastening for the present seems joyous, but grievous," Heb. xii. 11. At first, chastisement seems very bitter, but afterwards it yieldeth the peaceable fruits of righteousness unto them that are exercised thereby. The fruit of patience is not found at the first brunt, but after we are well exercised and acquainted with a suffering condition : affliction is the true moly ;* though the root be bitter, yet the fruit is sweet; there is meat in the eater, out of the strong comes sweetness ; and then when the soul begins to taste the sweet fruit which grows upon the bitter root, it says with the church in the Lamentations, "It is good that a man should both hope and quietly wait for the salvation of the Lord; it is good that a man should bear the yoke in his youth," Lam. iii. 26, 27. That is, I shall not be a loser by my sufferings, I see the fruit will abundantly compensate the smart of a suffering condition.

Thus, I say, one way or other, God works his children into a sweet obediential frame by their sufferings. Even of Christ himself, the Son of God by nature, it is said, "He learned obedience by the things which he suffered," Heb. v. 8. He came experimentally to know what it was to be subject to the will of his Father. It is most properly true of the adopted children, they learn obedience by the things which they suffer, and that not only in a passive but in an active sense. By *suffering* God's will we learn to *do* God's will. God hath no such obedient children as those whom he nurtures in the school of affliction. At length

* A herb.

C

God brings all his scholars to subscribe, *What God will, when God will, how God will: thy will be done on earth, as it is in heaven.* A blessed lesson!

4. A fourth lesson is, humility and meekness of spirit.

It is one of God's designs in affliction, to " hide pride from man," Job xxxiii. 17. to spread sack-cloth upon all his glory, that so man may see no excellency in all the creature wherein to pride himself. God led Israel forty years in the wilderness to humble them. By the thorns of the wilderness God pricked the bladder of pride, and let out the windiness of self-opinion that was in their hearts. Prosperity usually makes men surly and supercilious towards their poor brethren; " The rich answers roughly :" even while " the poor useth entreaties," (Prov. xviii. 23.) maketh his addresses to him with all humility and observance, he holds up his head, or turns his back upon him with scorn and con-tempt, and thinks himself too good to give his poor neighbour a soft and peaceable answer. They speak hard things ; these rough-cast Nabals, a man cannot tell how to speak to them. Pride is a humour which naturally runs in our veins, and it is nourished by ease and prosperity. And therefore to tame this pride of spirit that is in man, God takes him into the house of correction, puts his feet in the stocks, and there teacheth him to know himself: " He humbled thee, and suffered thee to hunger," Deut. viii. 3. Hunger brought down Israel's stomach, and did eat out that proud flesh which began to rankle. Hence it is that if you take the children of God either yet in, or newly come out of the furnace of affliction, you shall observe them to be the tamest, meekest creatures upon the earth; as it is said of the new convert, "A little child may lead them," Isa. xi. 6. Whereas before it may be they were so stiff and high in the instep, that an angel of God could not tell how to deal with them; now the meanest of God's ministers or servants may reprove and counsel, &c. "a little child may lead them." That David whom sin made so fierce that he put his poor Ammonitish prisoners and captives to death in cold blood, 2 Sam. xii. 31.* yea tormented them to death with saws, and harrows, and axes of iron; and burnt them alive in fiery brick-kilns; him did banishment and persecution make so tame, that not only the righteous might reprove him, but even the wicked might reproach him, Psa. cxli. 5. and he holds his peace, or if he speak, they be words of patience and submission: " So let him curse, because the Lord hath said, Curse David," 2 Sam. xvi. 10. A man by trouble comes to know his own heart, which in prosperity he was a stranger to; he seeth the weakness of his grace, and the strength of his corruption; how nothing is weak but grace, nothing strong but sin; and this lays him in the dust. Oh wretch that I am! And truly when a man hath learned this lesson, he is not far from deliverance. " Seek the Lord all ye meek of the earth, seek righteousness, seek meekness, it may be ye shall be hid in the day of the Lord's anger," Zeph. ii. 3. This is God's design, first, to meeken his people by affliction, and then to save them from affliction, Psa. cxlix. 4. For the Lord taketh pleasure in his people, he will beautify the meek with salvation.

* The Hebrew word means put them *to* saws, &c. and means no more than to employ them as slaves in the most menial occupation. *T. H. Horne.* Ed.

5. God by affliction discovers unknown corruption in the hearts of his people, " He led thee through the wilderness these forty years to humble thee, and to prove thee, to know what was in thy heart," Deut. viii. 2. that is, to make thee know what was in thy heart; what pride, what impatience, what unbelief, what idolatry, what distrust of God, what murmuring, what unthankfulness was in thy heart; and thou never tookest notice of it. I tell you christians, sin lieth very close and deep, and is not easily discerned till the fire of affliction comes and makes a separation of the precious from the vile. The furnace discovers the dross which lay hid before. " What shall I do," saith God, " for the daughter of my people ?" Jer. ix. 7. They are exceeding bad, and they know it not. " What shall I do with them ? I will melt them, and try them." Into the furnace they shall go, and there I will discover themselves to themselves, and show them what is in their hearts. In the furnace we see more corruption and more of corruption, than ever appeared or was suspected. Oh, saith the poor soul whom God hath taught in the school of affliction, I never thought my heart so bad as now I see it is, I could not have believed the world had had so much interest in my heart, and Christ so little; I did not think my faith had been so weak, and my fears so strong. I find that faith weak in danger, which I had thought had been strong out of danger. Little did I think the sight of death would have been so terrible, parting with nearest friends and dearest relations so piercing. Oh how unskilful and unwise am I to manage a suffering condition, to discern God's ends, to find out what God would have me to do; to moderate the violence of mine

own passions, to apply the counsels and comforts of the word for their proper ends and uses! Oh where is my patience, my love, my zeal, my rejoicing in tribulations! Ah! did I ever think to find my heart so discomposed, my affections so out of command, my graces so to seek when I should fall into divers temptations! What a deal of self-love, pride, distrust in God, creature-confidence, discontent, murmuring, rising of heart against the holy and righteous dispensations of God, is there boiling and fretting within me! Wo is me, what a heart have I!

And besides all this, in the hour of temptation, God brings old sins to remembrance. "We are verily guilty concerning our brother," Gen. xlii. 21. could Joseph's brethren say, twenty years after they had sold him for a slave, when they were in danger to be questioned for their lives, as they feared. And thus when the Israelites cry to God in their sore distress for rescue and deliverance, God puts them in mind of their old apostasies: " Ye have forsaken me, and served other gods, &c. go and cry to the gods whom ye have chosen," Judg. x. 13, 14. Suffering times are times of bringing sin to mind. " If they bethink themselves in the land whither they were carried captives," Heb. If they bring back to heart, 1 Kings viii. 47. Captivity is a time of turning in upon ourselves, and bringing back to heart our doings which have not been good in God's sight. Thus David under the rod could call himself to account, " I thought on my ways, and turned my feet," &c. Psa. cxix. 59.

This now is another lesson which God teacheth by affliction; and it is of great use to humble us, and to empty us out of ourselves, to make us fly to Jesus Christ for righteousness and strength, Isa. xlv. 24. In a word, God lets us see what is crooked that we may straighten it, what is weak that we may strengthen it, what is wanting that we may supply it; what is lame that it may not be turned out of the way, but that it may rather be healed.

6. In the school of affliction God doth teach us to pray. They that never prayed before will pray in affliction. "Lord in trouble they have visited thee, they poured out a prayer when thy chastening was upon them," Isa. xxvi. 16. They that kept their distance with God before, yea, that said to the Almighty, Depart from us, in their affliction can bestow a visit upon God; "In trouble they have visited thee:" and they that never prayed before, or at least did but now and then drop out a sleepy sluggish wish, can now pour out a prayer when chastisement is upon their loins. Rebels, fools, mariners, even the worst of men, can cry to God in their trouble, Psa. cvii. 11. 17. 23. The very heathen mariners fall to their prayers in a storm, and can awaken the sleepy prophet to this duty; "What meanest thou, O sleeper? arise and call upon thy God," Jonah i. 5, 6. Hence we use to say, "He that cannot pray, let him go to sea." Thus I say affliction opens dumb lips, and untieth the strings of the tongue to call upon God.

But whom God teacheth in affliction, they learn to pray in another manner—more frequently, more fervently.

They pray more frequently; God's people are vessels full of the spirit of prayer, and affliction is a piercer, whereby God draws it out. "For my love they are my adversaries, but I give myself unto prayer," Psa. cix. 4. David was always a praying man, but now under persecution he did nothing else. " I give myself unto prayer:" as wicked men give themselves up to their wickedness, so David gave himself up to prayer, he made it his work. Hence you may observe that most of the psalms are nothing else almost but the runnings out of David's spirit in prayer under variety of afflictions and persecutions ; as his troubles were multiplied, so his prayers did multiply. The hoiy man was never in that condition wherein he could not pray, &c. Alas, it is sad to consider that in our peace and tranquillity, we pray carelessly by fits and starts many times, we suffer every trifle to come and justle out prayer ; but in affliction God keeps us upon our knees, and, as it were, tieth the sacrifice to the horns of the altar.

And as he teacheth us to pray more frequently, so also to pray more fervently. Even of Christ himself it is said, that being in an agony he prayed more earnestly ; more intensively ; he prayed till he sweat again ; yea till he sweat great drops of blood, Luke xxii. 44. He sweltered out his soul through his body in prayer; the reason whereof was, because he had not only the pangs of death, but the sense of his Father's wrath to conflict withal : and so it is with believers many times ; outward afflictions are accompanied with inward desertions. So it was with David, Psa. xxii. and cxvi. 3, 4, &c. And then he gathers up all his strength to prayer, and like a true son of Jacob wrestleth with God, and will not let him go till he gets the blessing, Psa. cxliii. 6, 7, &c.

Truly, christians, those prayers wherewith you contented yourselves in the day of your peace and prosperity, will not serve your turn in the hour of temptation. Then you will call to mind your short, slight, cold, dead, sleepy, formal devotions in your families and closets, and be ashamed of them. Then you will see need of praying over all your prayers again, and stir up yourselves to take hold upon God, Isa. lxiv. 7. Indeed for this very end God sends his people into captivity that he may draw out the spirit of prayer, which they have suffered to lie dead within them. " Oh my dove that art in the clefts of the rock, in the secret places of the stairs; let me see thy countenance, let me hear thy voice, for sweet is thy voice, and thy countenance is comely," Sol. Song, ii. 14. Christ's dove never looks more beautiful in his eyes, than when her cheeks are bedewed with tears; nor ever makes sweeter music in his ears, than when she mourns to him, out of the rock, and from under the stairs, in a dark and desolate condition : then saith Christ, " Thy countenance is comely, and sweet is thy voice."

7. By correction God brings the children of promise into more acquaintance with the word. He teacheth them out of his law. As here : " It is good for me that I have been afflicted, that I might learn thy statutes." God sent David into the school of affliction, there to learn the statutes of God. By correction the people of God learn, 1. To converse with the word of God more abundantly. 2. To understand it more clearly. 3. To relish it more sweetly.

(1.) By affliction they come to converse with the word more abundantly. It is their duty at all times to study the word ; to let it dwell richly in them in all wisdom, Col. iii. 16. Job esteemed the words of God's mouth more than his necessary food. And it is their happiness as well as their duty; "Blessed is the man that walketh not in the counsel of the ungodly, but his delight is in the law of the Lord and in his law doth he meditate day and night." Psa. i. 1, 2. But what through distraction without, and distemper within, the children of God many times grow strangers to their bibles, they suffer diversions to interpose between the word and their hearts, and as they pray carelessly, so they read carelessly, and suffer their bibles to lay by the walls while they are taken up with other entertainments in the world. And therefore God is forced to deal with them as we do with our children, to whip them to their books by the rod of correction. " It is good for me that I have been afflicted, that I might learn thy statutes." When they are cast out by the world, then they can run to the word. "Princes did sit and speak against me ;" that is, they sat in counsel to take away his life, that they might condemn him as a traitor against Saul : and what did he in the mean time? it follows, " but thy servant did meditate in thy statutes." And again, "Princes have persecuted me without a cause, but my heart standeth in awe of thy word," Psa. cxix. 23. 161. While the persecutors are consulting with the oracles of hell to sin against David, David is consulting with the oracles of heaven, that he might not sin against God. " My heart standeth in awe of thy word :' while they sinned and feared not, David feared and sinned not.

(2.) They learn by affliction to understand the word more clearly. As it was with the disciples in reference to Christ's resurrection ; the resurrection of Christ was a lively comment upon the prophecies

of Christ : " These things understood not his disciples at the first, but when Jesus was glorified, then
remembered they these things," John xii. 16. that
is, they remembered them understandingly, they
remembered them believingly, they knew what they
meant. So it is with the people of God many times
in reference to affliction ; the rod expounds the
word, providence sometimes interprets the promise.
The children of God had never understood some
scriptures, had not God sent them into the school
of affliction : then they can remember how it is
written, &c. they can bring God's word and God's
works together.

(3.) Affliction makes them relish the word more
sweetly.   In prosperity many times we suffer the
luscious contentments of the world so to distemper
our palates that we cannot relish the word, taste no
more sweetness in it than in the white of an egg,
as Job speaks in another case.   But when God
hath kept them for weeks, and months, and years
it may be, fasting from the world's dainties, when
they are thoroughly hunger-bitten in the creature ;
then, " How sweet are thy words to my taste ! yea,
sweeter than honey to my mouth," Psa. cxix. 103.
They are the words which David spoke in his affliction, witness ver. 23, with 24. " Princes did sit and
speak against me, but thy servant did meditate in
thy statutes :" and what follows ? " thy testimonies
are my delight." And ver. 161, with 162. " Princes
have persecuted me without a cause, &c.   I rejoice
at thy word as one that findeth great spoil."   The
rod did sweeten the word.   It is my delight, my
joy, a nest of sweetnesses.   "The full soul loatheth
an honey-comb," Prov. xxvii. 7.   When we are
crammed with creature-comforts, we nauseate many

times the very word itself, which is sweeter than the honey or the honey-comb. "but to the hungry soul every bitter thing is sweet." Let God famish the world round about us, then how cordial is a word of scripture consolation! How precious are the promises! Oh, said a gracious woman reduced to great straits, I have made many a meal's meat upon the promises when I have wanted bread.

The word is never so sweet as when the world is most bitter; and therefore doth God lay mustard upon the teats of the world, that we might go to the breasts of the word, and there "suck and be satisfied with the milk of consolation," Isa. lxvi. 11. "This is my comfort in my affliction: for thy word hath quickened me," Psa. cxix. 50. Blessed be God for that correction which sweetens the word unto us.

8. God by bringing his people into troubles, especially if life-threatening dangers, doth show them the necessity of sound evidence for heaven and happiness. Alas, with what easy and slight evidences do we often content ourselves in the time of our prosperity, when the candle of the Almighty doth shine in our tabernacles! when all is peace and quiet round about us! The heart being taken up with other fruitions, we want either time or will to pursue the trial of our own estates. People mind only what will serve their turn for the present, and quiet their hearts, that they may follow their pleasures and profits with the less regret; and therefore to save themselves a labour, they take that for evidence which the sluggish carnal heart wisheth were so. But now in the hour of temptation, fig-leaves will cover nakedness no longer; nothing will

serve the turn but what will be able to stand before God and endure the trial of fire in the day of Christ. Oh then one clear and unquestionable evidence of interest in Christ, and the love of God, will be worth ten thousand worlds. Shadows and appearances of grace will vanish before the Searcher of hearts. It must be perfect love that will cast our fear, 1 John iv.18. Truth and soundness of grace only can give boldness in the day of judgment. Ah, what idle and deceitful hearts have we in the midst of us, that can take up with loose conjectures, go to the word and sacrament with those evidences, upon which we dare not venture to die? And yet good and upright is the Lord who will teach sinners his way, Psa. xxv.8; who, by the thunder-claps of his righteous judgments will awaken the vain creature out of those foolish dreams in which, if they should die, they were undone for ever. Well, let us be urging and pressing this question upon our own souls; Will this faith save me when I come to stand before the throne of the Lamb? Will this love give me boldness in the day of judgment? Will this evidence serve my turn when I come to die? Oh christians, let us be afraid to lie down with that evidence in our beds, wherewith we dare not lie down in our graves.

9. In the time of our trouble, God causeth us to see what an evil and bitter thing it is to grieve the good Spirit of God. When we are in the bitterness of our spirits and want the comforter, then we begin to call to mind how often we have grieved the Spirit, which would have been a comforter to us, and have sealed us up to the day of redemption; and say within ourselves, in reference to the Spirit of God, as some-

times the sons of Jacob said one to another in reference to Joseph; "We are verily guilty concerning our brother, in that we saw the anguish of his soul when he besought us, and we would not hear; therefore is this distress come upon us," Gen. xliii. 21. In some such language I say will the soul in the hour of temptation bespeak itself; Ah, I am verily guilty concerning that tender Spirit of grace and comfort, which hath often besought me as it were with tears, saying, "Oh do not this abominable thing which I hate," Jer. xliv. 4. but I would not hear. Is not this He whose rebukes I have slighted, whose counsels I have despised, whose motions I have resisted, whose warnings I have neglected, whose warmings I have quenched, yea, whose comforts I have undervalued, and counted them as a small thing? Ah wretch, how just is it now that the Spirit of God should withdraw! that he should despise my sorrows, and laugh at my tears; shut out my prayers, quench my smoking flax, and break my bruised reed! How just were it that He, whom I would not suffer to be a reprover in the day of my peace, should now refuse to be a repairer of my soul in the hour of my temptation! How righteous a thing were it that I, who so often have carried myself to his counsels, should now lie down in sorrow. Well, if the Lord shall please to bring my soul out of trouble, and to revive my fainting spirit with his sweet consolation, I hope I shall carry myself, for the future, more obediently to the counsels and rebukes of Jesus Christ in my soul, and hearken to the least whisperings of the Spirit of grace.

10. By chastisements, God draws the soul into sweet and near communion with himself. Outward

prosperity is a great obstruction to our communion with God. Partly because, by letting out our affections inordinately to the creature, we suffer the world to come in between God and our hearts, and so intercept that sweet and constant traffic and intercourse which should be between God and us. God's people offend most in their lawful comforts, because there the snare being not so visible as in grosser sins, they are the more easily taken; we are soonest surpised where we are least jealous. Partly also for want of keeping up our watch against lesser sins. While our hearts are warmed with prosperity, we think many times small sins can do no great harm; but herein we wofully deceive ourselves. For besides that the least sin hath the nature of sin in it, as the least drop of poison is poison; and that in smaller sins there is the greater contempt of God, in asmuch as we stand out with God for a trifle, (as we count it) and venture his displeasure for a little sensual satisfaction. I say, besides these and many other considerations which may render our small sins great provocations this is one unspeakable mischief, that small sins intercept our communion with God as much as great sins, and sometimes more. For whereas great sins by making deep wounds upon conscience, make the soul go bleeding to the throne of grace, and there to mourn and lament, never to give God rest till he gives rest to the soul, and by a fresh sprinkling of the blood of Christ, to recover peace and communion with God. Smaller sins not impressing such horror upon the conscience, are swallowed in silence with less regret, and so do insensibly alienate and estrange the heart from

Jesus Christ. The least hair casts its shadow; a barley-corn laid upon the sight of the eye will keep out the light of the sun, as well as a mountain. The eye of the soul must be kept very clear that will see God: " Blessed are the pure in heart, for they shall see God," Matt. v. 8. Little sins, though they do not disturb reason so much as great sins, yet they defile conscience, and the conscience under defilement (unlamented) is shy of God, and God shy of it.

But now affliction sanctified, as it doth deaden the heart to the world, so it doth awaken and make conscience tender towards sin; the soul is made sensible of her departures from God, and of the bitter fruits of that departure, and now begins to lament after God in Augustine's language; Lord, thou hast made my heart for thyself, and it is restless and unquiet till it can rest in thee; "Return unto thy rest, O my soul." The soul hath many turnings and windings, but with Noah's dove, it can find no place for the sole of its foot to rest on, till it return into the ark, from whence it came. And now when the soul hath been weather-beaten abroad, if God will please to put forth his hand, and take it into himself, when dearest relations are become strangers, as David complains, Psa. lxxxviii. 8. 18. if God come and give the soul a visit; when the poor creature is in darkness, and can see no light, then for God to lift up the light of his countenance, and shine in a gracious smile upon the soul, and say unto it, "I am thy Salvation," of what sweet and unspeakable refreshment and consolation is this to the afflicted spirit! And what a gracious condescension is this in God, that when the soul by prosperity hath waxed wanton against Christ, and sported itself in unspouse-like familiarities with strangers, Jesus Christ should send it into the house of correction, and there by the discipline of the rod correct and work out the wantonness of the flesh, and when he hath made it meet for his presence, take it into sweet and social communion with himself again ! Jer. iii. 1. This is stupendous mercy, goodness that cannot be paralleled in the whole creation !

11. God maketh affliction the exercise and improvement of grace. In prosperity grace many times lieth dead and useless in the soul, which affliction awakens and draweth forth into exercise: the winter of our outward comforts proves not seldom the spring of our graces. Frosts and snow do starve the weeds, and nourish the good corn. Though faith and patience be of an universal influence into the holy life, " The life I live in the flesh, I live by the faith of the Son of God," Gal. ii. 20. yet affliction giveth them their perfect work. Of the times of persecution it is said, " Here is the patience and faith of the saints," Rev. xiii. 10. that is, Now is the time for the saints of God to exert their faith and patience, and to let them have their perfect work. There is a work of patience, and there is a perfect work; " The trial of faith worketh patience," James i. 3, 4. that is, the sufferings whereby our faith is tried, as gold is tried in the furnace, it worketh, or, as the word signifieth, it perfecteth. The cross exerciseth, and exercise perfecteth the grace of patience : as sufferings arise, so patience ariseth also ; " Be patient, brethren, till the coming of the Lord," James v. 7. Do you bear the affliction till Christ come and take it off: let your patience be of the same extent with your

sufferings. As patience, so faith is not acted only but perfected by temptations. Sometimes the soul finds that faith lively in a suffering condition, which before it questioned whether it were alive or not; or if affliction do not find it lively, it makes it lively. The same furnace of affliction wherein God trieth our faith he doth refine it, and purifieth it more and more from the dross of infidelity. They are the purest acts of faith, which the soul puts forth in the dark. Faith never believes more than when it cannot see, because then the soul hath nothing to stay itself upon but God, Isa. l. 10. Sense while it seems to help, makes the work of faith difficult by doubling it: a man must first believe the insufficiency of what he seeth, before he can believe the all sufficiency of him that is invisible; "We look not at the things which are seen, but at the things which are not seen," 2 Cor. iv. 18. It is harder to live by faith in abundance than in want. The soul is a step nearer living upon God, when it hath nothing to live upon but God. Yea and when God is not seen he is most believed. "My God, my God, why hast thou forsaken me?" Psa. xxii. 1. Observe, and you shall find a great deal more of precious faith in that desertion, than of complaint. For, first, faith breaks forth, "My God," before forsaken. And again you have two words of faith for one of despair; "My God, my God, why hast thou forsaken me?" Faith speaks twice before sense can speak once. And third, faith speaks confidently and positively, Thou art my God. Sense speaks dubiously, Why hast thou? as if sense durst not call it a forsaking while faith dares say, "My God." Surely faith is never so much faith as in desertion. Faith's triumphs lie in the midst of despair, and even in this sense also; " Having not seen, yet believing, we rejoice with joy unspeakable and full of glory," 1 Pet. i. 8.

Godly sorrow, how is it enlarged by sanctified affliction ! while that stream, which was wont to run in the channel of worldly crosses, now is diverted into the channel of sin: "I will bear the indignation of the Lord, because I have sinned," Micah vii. 9. Any burden is light in comparison of sin, the very indignation of God. The soul that God teacheth by his chastisements can stand under the burden of God's indignation for sin, when it cannot stand under sin, which hath kindled that indignation. "Ah," crieth Job upon the dunghill, " I have sinned, what shall I do unto thee, O thou preserver of men!" He forgetteth his suffering in his sin ; he saith not, I have lost all my substance; I am now upon the dunghill as naked as ever I was born, save that I am clothed with wounds; my friends reproach me, my wife curseth me, or, which is worse, she bids me curse God. Satan persecutes me, and God himself is become mine enemy, &c. all this is befallen me ; what wilt thou do unto me, O thou preserver of men? but, " I have sinned, what shall I do unto thee ?" &c. Sufferings lead to sin, and sense of sin swalloweth up sense of sufferings. And what shall I say more ? the time would fail to instance in other graces, love, fear, holiness, &c. " By this shall the iniquity of Jacob be purged, and this is all the fruit to take away his sin," Isa. xxvii. 9. " He for our profit, that we might be partakers of his holiness," Heb. xii. 10.

Grace is never more grace than when besieged with temptations. The battle draws forth that fortitude and prowess, which in time of peace lay chilled in the veins for want of opposition and exercise. Tribulation worketh patience.

12. A twelfth lesson, which they learn in the school of affliction, is—The necessity and excellency of the life of faith.

(1.) The necessity of living by faith : where sense endeth, faith beginneth. "The vision is for an appointed time," Hab. ii. 3, 4. But what shall we do in the mean time? why, "the just shall live by faith ;" live by faith, or die in despair. When God pulls away the bulrushes of creature supports, the soul must either swim or sink. God teacheth this lesson, partly by the uncertainty of second causes, the vicissitudes that are in creature expectations ; a little hope to-day, to-morrow reduced to despair : good news to-day, Pharaoh says, Israel shall go ; bad news to-morrow, he rageth, and swears that if Moses see his face any more, he shall die, &c. Oh the ebbs and flows of sublunary hopes ! One speaks a word of comfort, another speaks words of soul-wounding terror ; now a parcel of good words, anon a threatening. The sick man is in hopes of reviving to-day, to-morrow at the point of death, What a woful heart-dividing life is a life of sense. a life which is worse than death itself, to be thus bandied up and down between hopes and fears, to be baffled to and fro between the may-bes of second causes ! to be like mariners upon the billows and surges of the tempestuous sea! "They mount up to heaven, they go down again to the depths ; their soul is melted because of trouble : they reel to and fro, and stagger like a drunken man, and are at their wits' end," (Hebrew ; All their wisdom is swallowed up,) Psa. cvii. 26, 27. And God teacheth the necessity of a life of faith partly by the disappointment of the creature. How often doth the creature totally fail, and abuse our expectation! like the deceitful brook, to which Job most elegantly compares his brethren, Job vi. 15, 16. which mocks the traveller, and when he comes for a draught of water to quench his thirst, sends him away with confusion and shame, ver. 20. "Surely men of low degree are vanity, and men of high degree are a lie," Psa. lxii. 9. Men of low degree would help, but cannot, there is vanity: and men of high degree can help many times, but will not; no, not when they have promised and sworn, there is a lie: both disappoint, the one by the necessity, the other by deceit; and disappointment is one of the greatest torments that a rational creature is capable of. Trust defeated causeth sorrow of heart, and confusion of face, Isa. xx. 5. and the stronger the confidence, the more shameful is the disappointment, Jer. xiv. 3. Agag comes forth singing, "Surely the bitterness of death is past," 1 Sam. xv. 32, 33. when behold he is going to his execution: both he and his hopes are hewn in pieces before the Lord. David himself looked on his right hand, and beheld, and there was no man that would know him. Peter-like, they knew not the man; they made as if they had never seen him before. So that churl Nabal says, "Who is David, and who is the Son of Jesse?" 1 Sam. xxv. 10. Some runagate, some idle fellow that hath broken away from his master, &c. And it was not Nabal only that stood at this distance from him; his nearest and dearest acquaintance cast him off: "Lover and friend hast thou put far from me, and mine acquaintance into darkness," Psa. lxxxviii. 18. "Refuge failed me, no man cared for my soul ;" or, as the Hebrew hath it, No man sought after my soul, Psa. cxlii. 3, 4. St. Paul was in no better condition in the persecution which befell him at Rome ; "At my first answer no man stood with me, but all men forsook me." Not a man of all them that sat under that famous apostle's ministry that would or durst appear to speak a word for him, or to him. O bitter disappointment, had not he had faith to support him under it ! And truly "such is our expectation, whither we flee for help to be delivered," &c. Isa. xx. 6. Sorrow and shame is the fruit of creature-expectation. But now on the contrary, "they looked unto the Lord, and were enlightened, and their faces were not ashamed," Psa. xxxiv. 5. Faith meets with no disappointment, God is always better than our expectation ; "Nevertheless the Lord stood with me, and strengthened me, &c. and I was delivered from the mouth of the lion," 2 Tim. iv. 17. By such experiences do we learn the necessity of living by faith. "I had perished in my affliction, unless thy law had been my delight ;" that is, unless David had learned to live by a promise, he had been but a dead man. Surely he dieth oft whose life is bound up in the dying creature : as oft as the creature fails, his hope fails, and his heart faileth ; when the creature dieth, his hope giveth up the ghost. He only lives an unchangeable life, that by faith can live in an unchangeable God.

We hear such things indeed in the word, but we believe them not till our own experience convinceth us of our infidelity. A long time do we stick totally in the creature, knowing no other life than that of sense and reason ; sacrificing to our own nests, and burning incense to our own drags : and because the word tells us much of living by faith, we would fain patch up a life between faith and sense, which indeed is not a life of faith. We do not live at all by faith, if we live not all by faith ; though we may use means, we must trust God, and trust him solely: and therefore, to bring us to this, God suffers us to be tired and vexed with the mockery of second causes ; and when we have spent all upon these physicians of no value, then, and never till then, we resolve for Christ. When David had experienced sufficiently the falseness and hypocrisy of Saul and his parasites, "They delight in lies, they bless with their mouth, but they curse inwardly," Psa. lxii. 4. then he resolves never to trust creature more: "My soul, wait thou only upon God, He only is my rock and my salvation," Psa. lxii. 5, 6. Unmixed trust in God is the fruit of our experience of the creature's vanity. We never resolve exclusively for God, till with the prodigal we are whipt home stark naked to our father's house. When the church had run herself, Jer. ii. 25. barefoot in following her lovers, who answered her expectation with nothing but fear, and sent her away with shame instead of glory, Isa. xx. 6. then she can go home, and, confessing her atheism and folly, gives up herself purely to Divine protection: "Asshur shall not save us; we will not ride upon horses: neither will we say any more to the work of our hands, Ye are our gods: for in thee the fatherless findeth mercy," Hos. xiv. 3.

(2.) By the mutability and disappointment of the creature, God teacheth his people the excellency of the life of faith. David, when he learned it in the school of affliction, wrote it and publisheth it for the use and benefit of after ages ; "Happy is he that hath the God of Jacob for his help, whose hope is in the Lord his God," Psa. cxlvi. 5. He had before, ver. 3. entered a caveat against creature-confidence, " Put not your trust in princes, nor in the son of man :" and gives the reason of it ; " There is no help or salvation in the best of men ; nor in the son of man, in whom there is no help." Alas, he is but a little breathing clay ; and when that breath goeth forth, he returns to his earth. When the breath is gone, there is nothing but a little lump of clay remaining ; " In that very day his thoughts perish." When the man dieth, all his counsels and plots and projects die with him. And having thus put in his caution against creature dependence, and given in the account of the vanity thereof, he shows the difference between trust in a dying man, and a living God. Trust in God is only able to make a man happy : they may seem happy, who have the great men of the world to trust to ; but he only is happy, who hath the God of heaven to trust to. " Blessed is he who hath the God of Jacob for his help." Why so ? Because, while they that trust in princes shall be disappointed, he that trusts in God shall never be disappointed : for, 1. He is Jehovah, whose hope is in the Lord, or in Jehovah his God, Isa. xxvi. 4. Jehovah, a fountain of beings : He gave a being to heaven and earth : " He made heaven and earth, the sea, and all that therein is," Psa. cxlvi. 6. and he that gave being to every crea-ture, can give being to his promise also. Can any thing be too hard for a creating God ? and as he can, so he will, for He keepeth truth for ever : " heaven and earth may pass away, but not one jot or one tittle of his promise shall pass away till all be fulfilled," Matt. v. 18. Men may prove unfaithful, but God will never prove unfaithful. He keepeth truth for ever: " Faithful is he that hath promised," Heb. x. 23. And thus the soul comes to see the sweetness and excellency of a life of faith, while others are mocked, and abused, and slain, by disappointment from the second causes : " He is kept in perfect peace, whose mind is stayed on God, because he trusteth in him," Isa. xxvi. 3. He liveth indeed, that liveth in Him to whom *always* is essential; who is The Eternal.

The excellency of a life of faith discovers itself in these four particulars :

[1.] It is a secure life. [2.] It is a sweet life. [3.] It is an easy life. [4.] It is an honourable life.

[1.] The life of faith is a secure life, the only safe life. " He shall dwell on high, his place of defence shall be in the ammunition of rocks." How securely doth he dwell, whose fortifications are impregnable, inaccessible rocks! rocks so high that none can scale them. In the Hebrew it is, He shall dwell in heights, or in high places: munition of rocks, or rocks so high that none can scale them ; rocks so thick that no breach can be made in them, rocks within rocks ; ammunition of rocks : and rocks so deep that none can undermine them. Surely a people or person rocked on every side, need not fear storming. *Objection.* But though rocks may be a good fence, they are but ill food, a man cannot feed on rocks ; rocky places are barren, though impregnable ; he may be starved, though he cannot be stormed ! no, the words following relieves that fear also, " Bread shall be given him ;" he shall have bread enough, and it shall cost him nothing ; it shall be given him ; and whereas a rock is but a dry situation, without either springs or streams, and thereupon a man might be exposed to perishing for want of water, thirst will slay as well as hunger; therefore it is likewise added. " His waters shall be sure."   He shall have waters which neither summer's heat nor winter's frost shall be able to dry up; never-failing waters shall fill his cisterns from day to day; " His waters shall be sure."   Under such an excellent metaphor is the security of a life of faith described; and this metaphor is expounded Isa. xxvi. 1. " Salvation will God appoint for walls and bulwarks."   Walls and bulwarks shall not be their salvation, but salvation their walls and bulwarks; how safely do they dwell who are walled about with salvation tself! the bulwarks are salvation, and that salvation is Jehovah; for so it follows, " Trust ye in the Lord for ever; for in the Lord Jehovah is everlasting strength;" or the Lord Jehovah is the Rock of ages.   His place of defence is the munition of rocks; and the Lord Jehovah is those Rocks, a Rock of ages.   Ages pass away one after another, but the Rock abides and abides for ever; " In the Lord Jehovah is everlasting strength."   He that rained manna in the wilderness, will give bread; and he that fetched water out of the rock, will be " a never-failing Fountain, his waters shall be sure."   Oh the security of a life of faith!

[2.] It is as sweet as it is safe.   Is it not a sweet thing to fetch all our waters from the fountain, from the spring head, before they be degenerated or mudded by the miry channel? Why, " All my fresh springs are in thee," saith faith to God, Psa. lxxxvii. 7.   Is it not sweet to be fixed and composed in the midst of all the mutations and confusions that are under the sun? Why this is the privilege of him that liveth by faith: "He shall not be afraid of evil tidings, his heart is fixed, trusting in the Lord," Psa. cxii. 7. And again; "Thou wilt keep him in perfect peace, whose mind is stayed on thee, because he trusteth in thee," Isa. xxvi. 3. Heb. Peace, peace; that is, multiplied peace; pure unmixed peace, constant and everlasting peace is the portion of him that liveth by faith, so far as he liveth by faith; unless sense and reason break in to disquiet, he liveth in a most sweet and immutable serenity.

[3.] It is an easy life. It is an easy life to have all provisions brought in to a man without any care or trouble; why, such is the privilege of a believer; he hath a support that supersedes all his cares. "In nothing be careful, but in every thing by prayer and supplication with thanksgiving let your requests be made known to God," Phil. iv. 6. Faith leaveth a believer nothing to do but to pray and give thanks; to pray for what he wants, and to give thanks for what he hath; that is all he hath to do. It is true, believers must labour and travail in the use of means, as well as the rest of the sons of Adam; but first, it is without care; "In nothing be careful;" without anxious heart-dividing, soul-distracting care. Oh, that is the thorn, the sting, which the sin of man and the curse of God hath thrust into all our labours, care and distraction; and this faith pulls out; so that now all the labour of faith is an easy labour, like the labour of Adam in Paradise. Faith useth means, but trusteth God; obediently closeth with the providence of means, but sweetly leaveth the providence of success to God. Yea, faith can trust God, when

there are no means to use, and say, " Although
the fig-tree shall not blossom, neither shall fruit be
in the vines, the labour of the olive shall fail, and
the fields shall yield no meat, the flock shall be cut
off from the fold, and there shall be no herd in the
stalls; yet I will rejoice in the Lord, I will joy in
the God of my salvation," Hab. iii. 17, 18.   Faith
can live upon God, when there is a famine upon the
whole creation.   The peace of God is as a court
of guard, to fence the heart from all surprises of
fear and trouble; " In nothing be careful, but in
every thing pray and give thanks, and the peace
of God which passeth all understanding shall keep
your hearts and minds through Christ Jesus,"
Phil. iv. 7.   As faith enjoyeth God in all things in
the greatest abundance, so she can enjoy all things
in God in the deepest want.

[4.] The life of faith is an honourable life.   It is
the honour of the favourite that he can go immediately to his prince when strangers must trace the
climax of court-accesses.   Yea, without all peradventure, it is an honourable life to live as God
himself liveth; and this is the glory of God, that
he liveth in himself and of himself; and truly in
their proportion such honour have all the saints.
They live in God and upon God here by faith; and
they shall life in God and upon God hereafter by
sight, in the beatifical vision.

This is the excellency of the life of faith, and
this the people of God experience by their sufferings; whereby God calls them out of the world,
and taking them into himself, he doth reveal to
them by degrees the mystery and privilege of living
upon God, and upon God alone.

13. By afflictions and distresses God takes us

off from self-confidence, and teacheth us to trust him more, and ourselves less. This is the same with the former, save only that we speak now of trust in God, in opposition to confidence in our-selves, and not in others ; a distemper that prevails much in our natures. Ever since we rendered ourselves able to do nothing, nothing but sin, we think ourselves able to do any thing : we fancy to ourselves a kind of omnipotence, when all our strength is to sit still. Naturally we are prone to entertain and nourish high presumptions of our own strength, and of our own wisdom.

(1.) Of our own strength. In our pros-perity we think ourselves able to carry any cross ; we fancy ourselves strong enough to carry away even Samson's gates upon our shoulders, and mettled to encounter any affliction in the world. But when the hour of temptation comes, we find we are but like other men, and are ready to sink with Peter, if but one wave riseth higher than another. Usually sufferings before they come are like a mountain at a great distance, which seems so small, that we think we could almost stride over it ; but upon nearer approaches, when we come to the foot of it, it appears insuperable, and looks so huge, as if it would fall upon us, and crush us in pieces. Peter is so big with love to Christ, that he will die with him, rather than forsake him ; yea though all the rest should betake themselves to their heels, he will stand by him to the last drop of blood ; and yet behold, when it comes to the trial, a weak silly damsel is able with a single question to fright him out of his confidence, and he doth not only forsake, but forswear his Lord. Pendleton, in the Book of Martyrs, says, he will fry out a fat body in flames of martyrdom, rather than betray his religion; but when the hour comes that Christ and religion have most need of him, he has not one drop of all that fat to spare for either.

(2.) As we are prone to presume of our own strength, so we are very apt to idolize our own wisdom; to lean to our own understanding, and think by our policy to wind ourselves out of any labyrinth of trouble and perplexity. But we find it otherwise; when we come into the snare, we then are forced to cry out with the church, " He hath hedged me about that I cannot get out, he hath made my chain heavy," Lam. iii. 7. Like a malefactor that hath broke prison; he thinks to run away, but he hath a heavy chain upon his heel, that spoils his haste; and being fenced in round about, he goeth to this corner, hoping to find some gap, but there he finds the hedge made up with thorns; and to another corner, and there also the briers stop him. Mark ye, that is not all; read on in the church's complaint, and you shall find greater obstructions: " He hath enclosed my ways with hewn stone," ver. 9. Suppose a man would venture the scratching of his flesh, to break through a hedge to save his life, " skin for skin, and all that a man hath will he give for his life," yet that would not do, God had taken away the hedge, and built a wall instead of it; a wall so high, that they could not clamber over; a wall so thick, that they could not dig through. The meaning is, man in affliction thinks to make his way through by his own art and cunning, but upon the attempt he finds difficulties arising still higher and higher, so that when all is done, escape is impossible, without an immediate rescue by the arm of omnipotence. This was Paul's case: "Our trouble which came to us in Asia, that we were pressed out of measure above strength, insomuch that we despaired even of life," 2 Cor. i. 8, 9. A great strait, (what it was in particular you may read Acts xix. from 22. so forward; in all probability it was that uproar at Ephesus, wherein Paul was like to have been pulled in pieces, for it was a trouble that befell him in Asia, ver. 8.) I say, it was a great strait, a strait wherein the apostle was at his wits' end and bereft of all counsel how to get out of the danger. As David complains, Psa. xiii. 2. "How long shall I take counsel in my soul!" that is, when he was persecuted by Saul, and beset with innumerable dangers, he took counsel, he thought of this means and the other means, cast about this way and that way, how to escape, but in vain, all his counsels left him as full of sorrow and despair as they found him. "How long shall I take counsel in my soul, having sorrow in my heart?" He had his sorrow for his pains. Thus it was with the apostle; all his counsel left him in the hand of despair: "We despaired even of life." His case was no other than the prisoner at the bar, at what time the sentence of death is passed upon him; he looks upon himself, and so do standers by, as a dead man; he is legally dead, dead to all intents and purposes of the law; there wants nothing but execution: why so it was with Paul; "We had the sentence of death in ourselves." The sentence was passed in his own breast; and now saith Paul, I am but a dead man. This was his strait, and it seemeth God had a plot in it, a design upon Paul; and what was that? himself will tell you; "We had the sentence of death in ourselves, that we should not trust in ourselves, but in God which raiseth the dead," ver. 9. See here, the design is expressed negatively and affirmatively. Negatively, that we might not trust in ourselves. God saw, even in that great apostle himself, a disposition to self-confidence, a proneness to be " exalted above measure, through the abundance of the revelations," 2 Cor. xii. 7. And therefore, as to prick the bubble of pride, God gave him a thorn in the flesh, &c. so, to work out this self-trust, God reduceth him to a state of despair, as to outward and visible probabilities ; " We had the sentence of death in ourselves, that we should not trust in ourselves ;" there is the negative branch of the design. And then the affirmative followeth, " But in God which raiseth the dead." By this desperate exigence God would teach Paul ever after where strength and counsel were to be had in the like extremities ; nowhere but in God, and in him abundantly. The God of resurrections can never be nonplussed ; he that can raise the dead, can conquer the greatest difficulty ; he that can put life into dead men, can put life into dead hopes, and raise up our expectations out of the very grave of despair : that God can put life into dead bones, is a consideration able to put life into a dead faith.

To this purpose it is very observable, that even those to whom God hath indulged the largest proportions of faith and courage, not only above other men, but above other saints ; yet even them God hath suffered not only to languish under fears, but even to despair under insuperable difficulties, before they could recover holy confidence in God. We find David, that great champion of Israel, more than once or twice surprised with dreadful fear: " I said in my haste," Psa. xxxi. 22. cxvi. 11.　The Hebrew signifieth, in my trembling, in my precipitancy; or as the septuagint translate it, in my ecstasy, when I was almost beside myself for fear.　Well, what did he say then? Why he said, " I am cut off from before thine eyes;" that is, God hath cast me out of his care, he looks no more after me, I am a lost man.　And again, " I said in my haste," in my passion, " all men are liars;" even Samuel himself, that told me I should be king; he hath seen but a false vision, and a lying divination; God never said so to him; no, " I shall one day fall by the hand of Saul."

And thus the prophet Jeremiah, Lam. iii. 57. " Thou drewest near in the day that I called upon thee; thou saidst, Fear not." But before God spake a fear not to his soul, he was afraid to purpose; hear what he saith, ver. 53, 54.　" They have cut off my life in the dungeon, and cast a stone upon me; waters flowed over mine head, then I said, I am cut off." Mark ye, with Paul, he had received the sentence of death in himself, he looks upon himself as a dead man, yea as already in his grave, and his grave-stone laid upon it; " They have cut off my life in the dungeon, and cast a stone upon me;" dead and buried, and a stone rolled to the mouth of the sepulchre.　And thus you may hear Jonah crying in the whale's belly, " I am cast out of thy sight," Jon. ii. 4.　And Zion, in the dust, tuning her lamentations.　" The Lord hath forsaken me, and my Lord hath forgotten me," Isa. xlix. 14.　Hezekiah reporting the sad discourses he had in his own bosom upon the sight of death, Isa. xxxviii, 9, 10, &c.　It were easy to multiply instances.

Why now this is continually our case, and this is still God's design. We are proud creatures, full of self-confidence; and therefore God by strange and unexpected providences doth hedge up our way with thorns, and wall up our path with hewn stones, brings to despair even of life, bereaveth us of counsel, deprives us of all our own shifts and policies, brings us under the very sentence of death; that we might not trust in ourselves, but in God which raiseth the dead. He overturns us by despair, convinces us of our impotence and folly, shows us what babes and fools we are in ourselves, that in all our future hazards and fears we might know nothing but God; "go in the strength of the Lord, and make mention of his righteousness, and of his only." And thus you see Peter, who before was so confident, that he thought all the world might forsake Christ sooner than himself, after he was convinced of his own infirmity and instability, when Christ, to put him in mind of his three-fold denial, put him upon that three fold interrogatory, " Simon Peter, lovest thou me more than these?" that is, than the rest of thy fellow-disciples, durst make no other answer but this, " Lord thou knowest;" he pleads nothing but his sincerity; and for that also he casts himself rather upon Christ's trial, than his own; " Lord, thou knowest."

14. By affliction God maketh himself known unto his people. How long do we hear of God before we know him? we get more by one practical discovery of God, than by many sermons: " I have heard of thee often by the hearing of the ear, but now mine eye seeth thee, therefore I abhor myself, and repent in dust and ashes," crieth Job upon the dunghill, Job xlii. 5, 6. In the word we do but

hear of God, in affliction we see him. Prosperity is the nurse of atheism; the understanding being clouded with the steams and vapours of those lusts which are incident to a prosperous estate, men grow brutish, and the reverence and sense of God is by little and little defaced. But now by affliction the soul being taken off from sense-pleasing objects, hath a greater disposition and liberty to retire into itself; and being freed from the attractive force of worldly allurements, the apprehensions are wont to be more serious and pregnant,* and so more capable of divine illumination. The clearer the glass is, the more fully doth it receive in the beams of the sun. When the warm breath of the world hath blown upon us, we are not so capable of the visions of God. The wicked through the pride of his heart will not know God ; " they say to the Almighty, Depart from us, for we desire not the knowledge of thy ways," Job xxi. 14. " Who is the Lord ?" saith Pharaoh. And truly the very godly themselves are exceedingly dark and low in their apprehensions of God ; our ignorance of God being never perfectly cured till we come to heaven, where we shall see him face to face, and know him as we are known. In the mean time, as by the strokes of divine vengeance God makes the wicked know him to their cost ; so by the rod of correction he makes his people to know him to their comfort. As God brought all his plagues upon Pharaoh's heart, that he might know who the Lord was in a way of wrath ; so he lays affliction upon the loins of his people, that they may know him in a way of love ; " Israel shall cry unto me, My God, we know thee." Moses never saw God so clearly, as when

* Clear, full.

he descended in a cloud, Exod. xxxiv. 5. And truly that dispensation was but a type of the method which God useth in making himself known unto his saints : He puts them into the clefts of the rock, covereth them with his hand while he passeth by, and then proclaimeth his name before them, The Lord, the Lord God, merciful and gracious, &c. The people of God have the most sensible experience of his attributes in their sufferings; his holiness, justice, faithfulness, mercy, all-sufficiency, &c.

(1.) His holiness. Affliction showeth what a sin-hating God, God is. For though his chastisements on his church be in love to their persons, they are in hatred to their corruptions; while he saveth the sinner he destroyeth the sin. " By this shall the iniquity of Jacob be purged, and this is all the fruit to take away his sin," Isa. xxvii. 9. If the soul live, sin must die.

(2.) His justice. Afflictions are correction to the godly, punishment to the wicked; in both God is righteous; thus Israel knew God, " Howbeit thou art just in all that is come upon us, for thou hast done right, but we have done wickedly," Neh. ix. 33. In the severest dispensations they judge themselves, and justify God; "Thou art just," &c. Yea when they cannot discern his meaning, they adore his righteousness; " Righteous art thou, O Lord, when I plead with thee; yet let me talk with thee of thy judgments; wherefore doth the way of the wicked prosper ?" Jer. xii. 1. When the soul is unsatisfied, God is not unjustified; " Righteous art thou, O Lord," &c.

(3.) His faithfulness. Faithfulness in the very affliction itself. " I know, O Lord, that thy judgments are right, and that thou in faithfulness hast afflicted me," Psa. cxix. 75. Faithfulness to his covenant ; for affliction is not so much threatened as promised to believers ; as Psa. lxxxix. 30—32. of which more hereafter. The more David was afflicted, the more God's faithfulness appeared. Oh, says the holy man, I would not have wanted a blow of all that discipline wherewith my heavenly Father hath chastised me.

Faithfulness in hearing prayer. "This poor man cried, and the Lord heard him, and saved him out of all his troubles," Psa. xxxiv. 6. I never lost a prayer by God : even when David wanted faith, God wanted not faithfulness. " I said in my haste, I am cut off from before thine eyes ; nevertheless thou heardest the voice of my supplications when I cried unto thee." God was faithful notwithstanding David's unbelief : " I said in my haste," &c. and he that believeth will not make haste ; " nevertheless thou heardest." Unbelief itself cannot make the faithfulness of God of none effect. I conceive that of the apostle 2 Tim. ii. 13. to bear this sense, " If we believe not, yet he abideth faithful, he cannot deny himself." It is not to be understood of a *state* of unbelief, but of an *act* of unbelief ; not of a want *of* faith, but a want *in* faith ; neither of which can render God unfaithful ; who is engaged not so much to our faith, as to his own faithfulness to himself, to hear the prayer of his troubled servants ; " Call upon me in the day of trouble, I will deliver thee, and thou shalt glorify me," Psa. l. 15.

This faithfulness of God believers do best experience in their sufferings : partly because then they are most prayerful. When our elder brother Esau is upon us, we can wrestle with our elder brother

Jesus, and not let him go till he bless us. And partly because then they are most vigilant to observe the returns of prayers: "My voice shalt thou hear in the morning, in the morning will I direct my prayer unto thee, and will look up," Psa. v. 3. In adversity we are early with God in prayer; "In the morning shalt thou hear my voice, in the morning will I direct my prayer;" it implieth double earliness, and double earnestness in prayer; in their affliction they will seek me early. And when we have done praying, we will begin hearkening; "I will look up." In prosperity we put up many a prayer that we never *look after;* God may deny or grant, and we hardly take notice of it. But in affliction we can press God for the returns of prayer; "Hear me speedily, O Lord, my spirit faileth, hide not thy face from me, lest I be like to them that go down into the pit;" not only denials, but delays kill us. Then we can hearken for the echo of our voice from heaven; "I will hear what God the Lord will say, for he will speak peace to his people," Psa. lxxxv. 8. As God cannot easily deny the prayer of an afflicted soul, so if he grant, we can take notice of it, and know our prayers when we see them again; this poor man cried, and the Lord heard him; and this endears the heart to God and to prayer: "I love the Lord, because he hath heard my voice and my supplications; because he hath inclined his ear unto me, therefore will I call upon him as long as I live," Psa. cxvi. 1, 2.

As faithfulness in hearing prayer, so also in making good the promise. The afflicted soul can witness unto God, "as we have heard, so have we seen," Psa. xlviii. 8. What we have heard in the promise, we have seen in the accomplishment.

God was never worse than his word. Affliction is a furnace, as to try the faith of God's people, so to try the faithfulness of God in his promises: and upon the trial, the church brings in her experience; "The words of the Lord are pure words, as silver tried in a furnace of earth, purified seven times," Psa. xii. 6. Let a man cast in the promise a thousand times into the furnace, it will still come out full weight: "As for God, his way is perfect, the word of the Lord is tried," Psa. xviii. 30. It is to be understood in both places of the word of the promise. A man may see heaven and earth upon a promise, and it will bear them up.

(4.) As affliction gives out the experience of God's faithfulness, so also of his mercy: mercy in the moderating of the chastisements: "In measure thou wilt debate with it," &c. Isa. xxvii. 8. In the midst of judgment he remembereth mercy, Hab. iii. 2. Even when God in his compassions saith of his afflicted church, "She hath received double of the Lord for all her sins," Isa. xl. 2. I have given her too many blows; in the sense of her own merits and his mercy she can reply, "No, Lord, thou hast punished us less than our iniquities deserve," Ezra ix. 13. Too much says God, too little saith the church. Oh blessed sight, thus to see God and the soul contending together! "It is of the Lord's mercies that we are not consumed, because his compassions fail not," crieth the church in Babylon; which denotes, it is banishment, it might have been destruction; we are in Babylon, we might have been in hell; and it is of the Lord's mercies, and his mercies alone, that we are not there. So saith the afflicted soul; if my burning fever had been the burning lake, if my prison had been the bottomless pit; if my banishment from society with friends had been expulsion, with Cain, from the presence of God, and that for ever; God had been righteous. It is never so bad with the people of God, but it might have been worse: any thing on this side hell is pure mercy.

And as mercy in moderating, so mercy in supporting. "When I said, my foot slippeth." Now I sink, I shall never be able to stand under this affliction, I cannot bear it. "Thy mercy, O Lord, held me up," Psa. xciv. 18. When David was sinking, God put underneath him his everlasting arms, and held him up, as Christ stretched forth his hand to save Peter when he began to sink. Even when God's suffering people are not sensible of any great ecstasies, yet then they find sweet supports; "His left hand was under me, his right hand embraced me." And yet it is not supporting mercy only which they experience in their sufferings, but not seldom his refreshing, his rejoicing mercy; so it follows, "In the multitude of my thoughts within me, thy comforts delight my soul," Psa. xciv. 19. My thoughts were dark and doleful, and full of despair, and not a few of them; multitudes brake in upon me, and even swallowed me up; but thy comforts were light and life, and delight to my soul: my thoughts did not sink me so deep, but thy comforts raised me up as high: my thoughts were a hell, but thy comforts were a heaven within me. The soul hears of God's mercy in prosperity, but it tastes of God's mercy in affliction, and, as it were oppressed with delights, can call to others, O taste and see how good the Lord is. Hence it is, that of all the days of the year, the apostle would choose, as it were, a Good Friday, a passion day, to rejoice in; "God forbid I should rejoice in any thing but in the cross of Jesus Christ."   Christ's sufferings for him, and his sufferings for Christ.

(5.) The all-sufficiency of God is the last attribute I mentioned, which God proclaims before his suffering people: " Now thou shalt see," saith God to Moses, " what I will do to Pharaoh," Exod. vi. 1. Hitherto thou hast seen what Pharaoh hath done to Israel, now thou shalt see what I can do to Pharaoh; and so they did see.   The doubling of their burdens was the dissolving of their bondage; the extinguishing of their line was the multiplying of their seed.   The same waters which were Israel's rocks were the Egyptians' grave; " I will pursue, I will overtake, I will divide the spoil; my lust shall be satisfied upon them: I will draw my sword, my hand shall destroy," Exod. xv. 9. so boasts the proud tyrant; I will, I will, I will, &c. nay, not so fast Pharaoh; let God speak the next word: "Thou didst blow with thy wind, the sea covered them, they sank as lead in the mighty waters," ver. 10. Oh sudden turn! there lieth Pharaoh and his six " I wills," and " I shalls," drowned in the sea. Thus did God appear to his oppressed Israel in the very nick of their extremities; " In the thing wherein they dealt proudly, God was above them," Exod. xviii. 11.   " And Israel *saw* that great work which the Lord did upon the Egyptians; and the people feared the Lord, and his servant Moses," Exod. xiv. 31.   Israel *saw;* in prosperity God works, but we see him not: affliction openeth our eyes; when we see our dangers, then we can see God in our deliverances.   God could have brought Israel to the land of promise a shorter cut, in forty days; but he leads them about in a howling

wilderness forty years, not a like place in all the world
to have starved them and their flocks: and why
but to proclaim to Israel, and all succeeding generations, that " man liveth not by bread alone, but
by every word that proceedeth out of the mouth of
the Lord doth man live?" Deut. viii. 3. Israel
learned more of God's all-sufficiency in a land of
drought, than they could have learned in the land
flowing with milk and honey, namely, that God
can feed without bread, and satisfy thirst without
streams of waters: that he can make the clouds
rain food, and the rock give out rivers: that the
creature can do nothing without God, but God can
do what he pleases without the creature.

Instances are endless: in a word, the suffering
time is the time wherein God makes his attributes
visible. "The Lord will be a refuge for the oppressed,
a refuge in time of trouble," Psa. ix. 9. and what
follows? "And they that know thy name, will put
their trust in thee," ver. 10. In the school of affliction
God reads lectures upon his attributes, visible lectures; and expounds himself unto his people: so
that many times they come to know more of God,
or more experimentally by half a year's sufferings,
than by many years' sermons.

15. God teacheth them in a suffering condition
to mind the duties of a suffering condition; to study
duty more than deliverance; seriously to inquire
what it is which God calls for under the present
dispensation. The soul crieth out with Paul, when
laid for dead at Christ's feet, "Lord, what wilt thou
have me to do?" Acts ix. 6. There is no condition
or trial in the world, but it gives a man opportunity for the exercise of some special grace, and the
doing of some special duty: and that is the work of

a christian, in every new state, and in every new trial, to mind what new duty God expects, what new grace he is to exert and exercise.

To mind deliverance only, is self-love, which is natural to man. " The captive exile hasteneth that he may be loosed, and that he should not die in the pit," &c. Man in affliction would fain be delivered, have the burden taken off, the yoke broken ; men make more haste to get their afflictions removed than sanctified : but this is not the work God looks for ; no, nor to think only what a man would do if he were delivered. Oh, thinks a man, if God would heal me of this sickness, deliver me out of this distress, I would walk more close with God, I would be more abundant in family-duties, I would be more fruitful in my converse ; I would do thus and thus, &c. Why now I say, though men should sit down in their afflictions, consider their ways, and make new resolutions for better things, if God shall give better times ; yet if this be all, it may be nothing else but a wile of the deceitful heart, a temptation and snare of the devil, to gain the time as it were of God ; a mere diversion to turn aside the heart from the present duty which God expects. And therefore when God intends good and happiness to the soul by the present chastisement, he pitcheth the soul upon the present duty, which is to " hear the rod, and who hath appointed it," Mic. vi. 9. to discern God's aim, and to find out the meaning of the present dispensation : to say to God, " I have born chastisement, I will not offend any more : that which I see not teach thou me, and if I have done iniquity, I will do no more," Job xxxiv. 31, 32. To reflect upon our ways and spirits, to complain of sin, and not of punishment ; " Wherefore doth a

living man complain? a man for the punishment
of his sin? Let us search and try our ways, and
turn again to the Lord," Lam. iii. 39. To think the
present condition the best: "I have learned in
whatsoever state I am, therewith to be content,"
Phil. iv. 11. In our patience to possess our souls,
Luke xxi. 19. to rejoice in God; yea to rejoice in
tribulation. Rom. v. 2, 3. To mind the public
calamities of the church more, and our private sufferings less: to pray for the welfare of Zion; "In
thy good pleasure do good unto Zion," Psa. li. 18.
To lift up Jesus Christ, and to make him glorious
by our afflictions; "That Christ may be magnified
in our bodies, whether it be by life, or by death,"
Phil. i. 20. Paul studied more how to adorn the
cross, than to avoid it; how to render persecution
amiable; and if he must suffer for Christ, yet that
Christ might not suffer by him; that Christ might
be exalted, and the church edified, Col. i. 24. This
God taught him; "I have learned," &c. And
lastly, to "commit the keeping of our souls to
God in well-doing, as unto a faithful Creator,"
1 Pet. iv. 19.

16. The sixteenth lesson is like unto it; and
that is, the privilege of a suffering condition. In
the school of affliction, one lecture which the Holy
Ghost readeth is, the fruits and advantages of a suffering condition. There is in every state of life a
snare and a privilege; and it is the folly and misery
of man left to himself, that he willingly runs into
the snare, and misseth of the privilege: he is only
able to add to his own misery, and to make his
condition worse than he finds it. Those whom God
loveth, he teacheth; he teacheth them to study, as
the duty of their present state, so the advantage.

When God takes away creature comforts, he doth not only necessitate, but by the secret impressions of love upon the heart, he emboldens the soul to look out for reparations, and to urge God for a recruit in some richer accommodations : " Lord," saith Abraham, " what wilt thou give me, seeing I go childless?" Gen. xv. 2. God had denied Abraham a child, and He must make Abraham amends for it. In the like manner, Lord, what wilt thou give me, saith a suffering saint, since I go wifeless, and friendless, and landless, and houseless? &c. yea Lord, what wilt thou give me, since I go ordinanceless, sermonless, sacramentless? &c. So the disciples, " Behold, we have forsaken all and followed thee, what shall we have therefore?" Matt. xix. 27. Faith may be a loser *for* Christ, but will not be a loser *by* Christ ; and accordingly Christ maketh an answer of faithfulness to this demand of faith " Verily I say unto you, there is no man that hath left house, or brethren, or sisters, or father, or mother, or children, or lands, for my sake, and the gospel's, but he shall receive a hundredfold now in this time," &c. Mark x. 29, 30. Advantage enough ; a hundred for one was the best year that ever Isaac had, Gen. xxvi. 12. But how shall this be made good? why, with persecution ; " Houses, and brethren, and sisters, and mothers, and children, and lands, *with persecution.*" Persecution must make up the account. It is very observable, that year wherein Isaac received his hundredfold was Isaac's suffering year ; the year wherein famine had banished him from his own country to sojourn with Abimelech in Gerar, Gen. xxvi. 1. Isaac's best harvest was in a year of famine : and this was typical to all the children of promise ; they must receive Isaac's increase upon Isaac's account, a hundredfold with persecution. And I conceive our Saviour may allude to this type, in this promise: In persecution the people of God find their hundredfold; when they make a scripture inquiry, they find sufferings, especially those for Christ's sake, to be their letters testimonial for heaven, Luke xxi. 13.

The pledge of adoption, Heb. xii. 6, 7.—A purifier for corruption, Isa. xxvii. 9.—The improvement of holiness, Heb. xii. 10.—A fining pot to faith, 1 Pet. i. 7.—Communion with Christ. The presence of the Spirit of God and of glory, 1 Pet. iv. 13, 14.—The church's treasury, Col. i. 24.—Weak christian's strength. Strong christian's confidence, Phil. i. 13, 14. In both, the gospel's advantage.—And lastly, the enhancement of glory, 2 Cor. iv. 17, 18. Here is the hundredfold with advantage.

In a word, whatever the affliction be, that it shall be the soul's gain; " All things work together for good to them that love God," Rom. viii. 28. This God teacheth his people: it is the very design of the eighth chapter to the Romans, and of the twelve first verses of the twelfth chapter to the Hebrews, to show that God's rod and God's love go both together. And this is a sweet and blessed lesson indeed; for this quiets the heart, and supports the soul under its burden. " For this cause we faint not;" why? Because "though our outward man perisheth, yet the inward man is renewed day by day," 2 Cor. iv. 16. which means, what we lose in our bodies we gain in our souls : what we lose in our estates we get in grace ; thus they bear up and comfort themselves in their deepest sorrows, while they that lie poring upon their afflictions, and are combining only to aggravate every circumstance of a suffering condition, sink their own spirits, vex their souls, dishonour God by slandering his dispensations ; and bring up an evil report upon the cross of Jesus Christ.   The spiritual privileges of God's suffering people, are therefore called " the peaceable fruits of righteousness," Heb. xii. 11. because the taste of this fruit brings in such peace and comfort into the soul, as makes it rejoice not in God only, but in tribulation, and in all these things to account itself " more than conqueror through him that hath loved us," Rom. viii. 37.

17. A lesson which God teacheth by his chastisements, is that which Christ taught Martha, namely, what is the one thing necessary ; affliction discovereth how much we are mistaken about our *must be's,* our *necessaries.* In our health, and strength, and liberty ; we think this thing *must be* done, and that thing *must be* done.   We think riches necessary, honours necessary, and a name in the world necessary ; we must get estates, and we must lay up large portions for our children, and we must raise our families, and call our lands after our own names, and the like, Psa. xlix. 11.   But in the day of adversity, when death looks us in the face, when God causeth the horror of the grave, the dread of the last judgment, and the terrors of eternity to pass before us, then we can put our mouths in the dust, smite upon our thigh, and sigh with the breaking of our loins, Oh how have I been mistaken! how have I fed upon ashes, and a deceived heart turned me aside, so that I could not deliver my soul, nor say, Is there not a lie in my right hand? Isa. xliv. 20. Fool, how have I been deceived,

and made the *bye* the *main*, and the *main* the *bye*. Then we can see that pardon of sin, interest in Christ, evidence of that interest, sense of God's love, a life of grace, and assurance of glory, &c. are the only indispensables. In a word, that Christ alone is the one thing necessary, and that all other things, at the best, are but *may-be's*. Yea, but loss and dung in comparison of the excellency of the knowledge of Christ Jesus the Lord, and of interest in him, and in his righteousness, Phil. iii. 8, 9. without which the soul is undone to all eternity. And therefore, O that christians would be wise, that they would not "spend their money for that which is not bread, nor their labour for that which satisfieth not," Isa. lv. 2. but labour for faith which might realize and substantiate unseen and spiritual things, Heb. xi. 1. and give them a being to the soul. They that will not learn this lesson in the school of the word, shall learn it in the school of affliction, if they belong to God; and therefore set your heart to it.

18. Time-redemption is another lesson which God teacheth those whom he corrects. In our tranquillity, how many golden hours do we throw down the stream, which we are like never to see again; for one whereof the time may come, when we would give rivers of oil, the wealth of both the Indies, mountains of precious stones, if they were our own, and yet neither would they be found a sufficient price for the redemption of any one lost moment! It was the complaint of the very moralist, and may be much more our complaint, Who is there among us, that knows how to value time, and prize a day at a due rate? Most men study rather how to pass away their time than to redeem it; prodigal of their

precious hours, as if they had more than they could tell what to do withal: our season is short, and we make it shorter. How sad a thing is it to hear men complain, O what shall we do to drive away the time?

Alas, even sabbath-time, the purest, the most refined part of time, a creation out of a creation, time consecrated by Divine sanction, how cheap and common is it in most men's eyes, while many do sin away, and the most do idle away those hallowed hours! Seneca was wont to jeer the Jews for their ill husbandry, in that they lost one day in seven, meaning their sabbath: truly it is too true of the most of christians, they lose one day in seven, whatever else; the sabbath for the most part is but a lost day; while some spend it totally upon their lusts, and the most, I had almost said the best, do fill up the void spaces and intervals or the sabbath from public worship, with idleness and vanity! But oh, when trouble comes, and danger comes, and death comes; when the sword is at the body, the pistol at the breast, the knife at the throat, death at the door, how precious would one of those despised hours be! Evil days cry with a loud voice in our ears, Redeem the time: that caution was written from the tower in Rome. "Redeeming the time because the days are evil," Eph. v. 16. In life-threatening dangers, when God threatens, as it were, that time shall be no more, Rev. x. 6. then we can think of redeeming time for prayer, for reading, for meditation, for studying and clearing out our evidences for heaven, for doing and receiving good, according to opportunities presented; yea, then we can gather up the very broken fragments of time, that nothing may be lost. Then God teacheth the soul what a choice piece of wisdom it is for christians, if it were possible, to be before hand with time; for usually it comes to pass through our unskilfulness and improvidence, that we are surprised by death; and we that reckoned upon years —many years—yet to come, have not, possibly, so many hours to make ready our accounts. It may be, this night is the summons, and then if our time be done, and our work to be begun, in what a case are we! The soul must needs be in perplexity at the hour of death, that seeth the day spent, and its work yet to do. A traveller that seeth the sun setting when he is but entering on his journey, cannot but be aghast: the evening of our day, and the morning of our task, do not well agree together; that time which remaineth is too short to lament the loss of by-past time. By such hazards God doth come upon the soul as the angel upon Peter in prison, and smites upon our sides, bids us rise up quickly, and gird up ourselves, and bind on our sandals, &c. Acts xii. 7. that we may redeem lost opportunities, and do much work in a little time; it is pity to lose any thing of that which is so precious and so short, 1 Cor. vii. 29.

19. Another lesson is how to estimate, at least to make some remote and imperfect guess at the sufferings of Jesus Christ, Lam. i. 12. In our prosperity we pass by the cross, that is, carelessly and regardlessly: at the best we do but shake our heads a little. The reading of the story of Christ's passion stirs up some compassion towards him, and passion against his persecutors; but it is quickly gone: we forget as soon as we get into the world again: but now let God pinch our flesh with some sore affliction; let him fill our bones with pain, and

set us on fire with a burning fever; let our feet be hurt in the stocks, and the irons enter into our souls; let our souls be exceedingly filled with the scorning of those that are at ease, and with the contempt of the proud ; let us be destitute, afflicted, tormented, &c. then happily we will sit down, and look upon Him whom we have pierced, and begin to say within ourselves, And are the chips of the cross so heavy? what then was the cross itself, which first my Redeemer did bear, and then it did bear him!   Are a few bodily pains so bitter? what then were those agonies which the Lord of glory sustained in his soul! Is the wrath of man so piercing? what was the wrath of God, which scorched his righteous soul, and sweltered his very heart blood through his flesh in a cold winter's night, so that his sweat was as great drops of blood, trickling down to the ground! Are the buffetings of men so grievous? what were the buffetings of Satan, which our Lord sustained, when all the brood of the serpent lay nibbling at the heel of his passion!   Is a burning fever so hot? how then did the most searching flames scald my Saviour's spirit! Is it such a heart-piercing affliction to be deserted of friends? what was it then for him, who was the Son of God's love, the darling of his bosom, to be deserted of his Father, which made him cry out to the astonishment of heaven and earth, " My God, my God, why hast thou forsaken me?"   Is a chain so heavy, a prison so loathsome, the sentence and execution of death so dreadful, oh what was it for him who made heaven and earth to be bound with a chain, hurried up and down from one unrighteous judge to another, mocked, abused, spit upon, buffeted, reviled, cast into prison, arraigned, condemned, executed in a most shameful and an accursed manner! Oh what was it for him to endure all this contradiction of sinners, rage of the devil, and wrath of God, in comparison of whom the most righteous person that ever was may say with the good thief on the cross, "And we indeed justly, but He, what evil hath he done?" "He made his grave with the wicked, and with the rich in his death, because he had done no violence, neither was any deceit in his mouth," Isa. liii. 9. Blessed be God, my prison is not Tophet, my burnings are not unquenchable flames, my cup is not filled with wrath : in a word, this is not hell. Blessed be God for Jesus Christ, by whom I am delivered from wrath to come, 1 Thess. i. 10. And thus, as the Lord Jesus, by the sensible experience of his own passion, came perfectly to understand what his poor members suffer while they are in the body, so we, by the remainders of his cross, which he hath bequeathed us as a legacy, come in some measure to understand the sufferings of Christ; or at least, by comparing things of such vast disproportion, to guess at what we cannot understand.

20. The last lesson which God teacheth by affliction is, how to prize and long for heaven. In our prosperity, when the candle of God shines in our tabernacles, when we wash our steps in butter, and the rock poureth us out rivers of oil, Job xxix. 6. we could sit down with the present world, and even say with the disciples, though not upon so good an account, "It is good for us to be here; let us here build us tabernacles." While life is sweet, death is bitter ; and heaven itself is no temptation, while the world gives us her friendly entertainments. But when poverty and imprisonment, reproach

and persecution, sickness and sore diseases, do not only pinch but vex our hearts with variety of aggravations, we are not so fond of the creature, but we can be content to entertain a parley with death, and take heaven into our considerations. Not that merely to desire to be in heaven, because we are weary of the world, is an argument of grace, or a lesson that needs Divine teaching; self-love will prompt as much as that comes to. But because, like foolish travellers, we love our way though it be troublesome, rather than our country! God by this discipline taketh off our hearts by degrees from this present world, and maketh us look homeward: being burdened we groan, 2 Cor. v. 4. and with the dove, we return to the ark when the world is afloat round about us? When David was driven from his palace, then, "Wo is me that my pilgrimage is prolonged :" so the Septuagint renders it. We should be contented, like the Israelites, with the garlick and flesh-pots of Egypt, if God did not set cruel taskmasters over us to double our burdens. When God hath thus lessened our esteem of the world, he discovers to us the excellency of heavenly comforts, and draws out the desires of the soul to a full fruition : When shall I come and appear in thy presence? Even so come, Lord Jesus. Affliction puts heaven into all those notions which make it heaven indeed.

To the weary it is rest, Isa. lvii. 2. Rev. xiv. 13. —To the banished it is home, 2 Cor. v. 6.—To the scorned and reproached it is glory, Rom. v. 2.—To the captive it is liberty, Rom. viii. 21.— To the conflicting soul it is conquest, Rom. viii. 37. —And to the conqueror it is a crown of life, Rev. ii. 10. Righteousness, 2 Tim. iv. 8. Glory, 1 Pet.

v. 4.—To the hungry it is hidden manna, Rev. ii. 17.—To the thirsty it is the fountain and waters of life, and rivers of pleasure, Rev. xxii. 17. Psa. xxxvi. 8, 9.—To the grieved soul, whether with sin or sorrow, it is fulness of joy; and to the mourner it is pleasures for evermore, Psa. xvi. 11.—In a word, to them that have lain upon the dunghill, and kept their integrity, it is a throne, on which they shall sit and reign with Christ for ever and ever, Rev. iii. 21. xxii. 5.

Surely, beloved, heaven thus proportioned to every state of the afflicted soul cannot fail to be very precious; and will make the soul with a stronger or weaker impulse, desire to be dissolved and to be with Christ, which is best of all, Phil. i. 23. A christian indeed is comforted by faith, but not satisfied; or if satisfied, it is in point of security, not of desire: because here " we are absent from the Lord, and walk by faith, not by sight," 2 Cor. v. 6, 7. Hope, though it keep life in the soul, yet it is not able to fill it: he longs and thinks every day a year till he be at home in his Father's arms, and sit down on his Father's throne, crowned with his Father's honour and glory. They that walk by faith cannot be quiet till they be in the sight of those things which they believe. Jacob when he heard that Joseph was alive, though he did believe it, yet could not be satisfied with hearing of it; but saith he, "I will go and see him before I die:" so the believing soul, He, whom my soul loveth, was dead, but is alive, and behold he liveth for evermore, Rev. i. 18. I will die that I may go and see him: as Augustine, upon that answer of God to Moses, " Thou canst not see my face, and live," Exod. xxxiii. 20. makes this quick and sweet reply, " Then, Lord, let me die that I may see thy face."

Thus I have presented you with those twenty several lessons which Jesus Christ, the great Prophet of his church, teacheth his afflicted ones to take out in the school of affliction. And now, as I told you in my entrance upon this subject, all these lessons may be reduced to three great summary, comprehensive instructions.

First. The sinfulness of sin.

Second. The emptiness of the creature.

Third. The fulness of Jesus Christ.

The first summary comprehensive lesson, is the sinfulness of sin. Sin is always very sinful; but in our prosperity we are not so sensible of it: the dust of the world doth so fill our eyes, that we cannot make a clear and distinct discovery of the evil that is in sin: but now, by the sharp and bitter waters of affliction, God doth wash out that dust, and clears the organ to make a perfect discovery, and to discern sin, as it is, and not as usually it doth appear: sin becomes exceeding sinful, Rom. vii. 13. God hath four glasses, wherein he discovers to the soul the evil that is in sin ; 1. The glass of the law, James i. 23, 24. 2. The blood of Christ, Rev. i. 5. 3. Afflictions and chastisements in this present world, Lam. iii. 39. 42. 4. The torments of hell, Matt. xxv. 41.

Indeed of all these glasses, the blood of Christ is the clearest, and doth most fully and perfectly represent the exceeding sinfulness that is in sin, the stain and spot whereof could be washed out with no other element but the blood of the Son of

God; for, as it was purchasing blood, so it was expiating blood. " He hath loved us, and washed us with his own blood," Rev. i. 5. But though this be the purest glass, yet God doth make frequent and great use of the third glass also—afflictions and chastisements for sin, to discover to the children of promise the greatness of that evil which is in sin. It is very notable how God brings the Israelites this glass in their affliction, and bids them, as it were, see their face in it. " Know therefore and see, that it is an evil and bitter thing that thou hast forsaken the Lord thy God, and that my fear is not in thee, saith the Lord God of hosts," Jer. ii. 19. In this glass he discovers to them a fourfold evil in sin.

(1.) As it is the cause of all other evils of punishment. " Hast thou not procured this unto thyself, in that thou hast forsaken the Lord thy God?" &c. Jer. ii. 17. He bids them read all their sins in their punishments; he bids them look upon sin as a mother-evil, that hath all other evils in it; which means, Thank thyself for all the affliction that is upon thee; thou hast procured this unto thyself. Art thou in captivity, in prison, in distress, &c. thank thy idolatry, and thy adulteries, whereby thou hast forsaken the Lord thy God. Thank thyself for all the misery that is upon thee. Every man's heart may say to him as Apollodorus's heart cried to him out of the boiling caldron: I have been the cause of all this. As lust when it hath conceived, brings forth sin, so sin when it is finished, when it is perfected, will bring forth death, James i. 15. Sin is the child of lust, and the mother of death.

(2.) In this glass God represents sin to their view, as an evil in itself: " Know therefore and see that it is an evil thing and bitter;" that sin doth not only bring evil, but is evil; it is an evil thing: not only that it works bitterness, but is bitterness; it is a bitter thing: it hath a bitter root, as well as it brings forth bitter fruits. God leads the sinner by affliction to take notice not only what sin doth, but what sin is; it is evil. Yea,

(3.) That it is a pure, unmixed evil. It is an evil thing, the whole being of sin is evil. In the evil of affliction there is some good, for it hath God for the author. "Is there an evil in the city, and the Lord hath not done it?" Amos iii. 6. And it hath good for its end: "All things shall work together for good to them that love God," Rom. viii. 28. "It is good for me," saith David, "that I have been afflicted," Psa. cxix. 71. But now sin is a simple uncompounded evil, for it hath the devil for the author; "He that committeth sin is of the devil," 1 John iii. 8. and death for its end; "The wages of sin is death," Rom. vi. 23. death in its vastest comprehension, sin is evil all over.

(4.) The glass represents it yet worse, and that is, as it is an evil against God. It is a departure from God, "Thou hast forsaken the Lord thy God," Jer. ii. 17. and so again, ver. 19. "Thou hast forsaken the Lord thy God; my fear is not in thee." Sin, as the schools define it, is an aversion from God, and a conversion or turning to the creature. "My people have committed two evils; they have forsaken me the fountain of living waters, and hewed them out cisterns, broken cisterns that can hold no water," ver. 13. Sin is not only an unmixed evil, but a twisted multiplied evil. It is a departure from the fountain of life and glory, and a turning to a scanty, and a broken vessel, which leaks out as fast as it is poured in. Now here is the exceeding sinfulness of sin, that it is an evil against God ; punishment is but an evil against the creature : thou hast procured this unto thyself, affliction is but a contradiction to the will of the creature ; but sin is a contradiction to the will of God. Whence we may safely conclude, that there is more evil in the least sin, than there is in the greatest punishment, even hell itself; the hell that is *in* sin, is worse than the hell that is prepared *for* sin. Yea and behold one evil more in this glass, the aggravation of all the rest, and that is,

5. That sin is a causeless evil, a causeless departure, "Thou hast forsaken the Lord thy God, when he led thee by the way," Jer. ii. 17. when he led thee as a guide to direct thee, led thee as a stay to support thee ; he put underneath thee his everlasting arms : he led thee as a convoy to guard thee, and led thee as a Father to provide for thee. Thou wantedst nothing, and yet thou hast forsaken the Lord thy God. This is the aggravation ; " O generation," (generation of what? why of what you will; God leaves a space, as it were, that we may write down what we please; generation of vipers, generation of monsters, any thing, rather than the generation of his children :) " O generation, see ye the word of the Lord." Still he holds the glass before their eyes, and what are they to behold there ? Why their causeless apostasy and rebellions ; for so it follows, " Have I been a barren wilderness, a land of darkness ? have ye wanted any thing ? wherefore then say my people, We will come no more unto thee ?" ver. 31. O this departure is causeless and wilful. God saith to the sinner, as Pharaoh said to Jeroboam, when he would be gone from him, " But what hast thou lacked with

me, that behold thou seekest to be gone from me?"
1 Kings xi. 22, and the sinner seemeth to answer God
as Jeroboam there answered Pharaoh: " Nothing,
howbeit let me go in any wise." Jeroboam could
come to Pharaoh when he was in distress; but,
when the storm was over at home, he will be gone
again, though he cannot tell why: and so deals the
treacherous heart with God; and this causeless
departure from God is a high aggravation of sin:
God is often upon it, as Isa. i. 2, and Amos vi. 3—
5, &c. The soul sinneth only because it will sin;
in a word, affliction is one of God's tribunals
where the sinner is arraigned, convicted, and condemned: " As many as I love, I rebuke and chasten ;"
the Greek words signify to convince and correct,
that is, by correction to convince of sin, Rev. iii. 19.
Truly, in affliction, sin is laid open before a man's
eyes in such sort as he is enforced to plead guilty.
God sits as judge; conscience is witness, a thousand
witnesses; sin the indictment; affliction both evidence and execution. Hence it is, that, sooner or
later, the convinced soul sees sin a greater evil
than affliction, whatever it is; and now, as it were,
forgetting the affliction, begins to mourn only for
sin, crying out with holy Job in the dust, " I have
sinned; what shall I do unto thee, O thou Preserver
of men?" Job vii. 20. He saith not, My substance is spoiled, my children destroyed, my body is
become filled with loathsome diseases, and myself
a terror to myself and standers by, what wilt thou
do unto me, O thou Preserver of men? but, " I have
sinned; what shall I do unto thee," &c. Affliction
led him to sin; correction was made conviction,
and sin now lieth heavier upon him than all his
sufferings. This is the first comprehensive lesson.

Second. The emptiness of the creature.

In our prosperity we stick in the creature, and dote upon the creature, the things and persons in this present world, as if there our happiness and comfort were bound up: but in the day of adversity, God convinceth us of our mistakes, by causing us to see the emptiness and vanity of all sublunary contentments; we begin to find the world to be but gilded emptiness, a mere nothing. Then ask the soul what it thinks of the world and all the elements thereof, the lusts of the flesh, the lusts of the eyes, and the pride of life, as the apostle sorts them, which formerly did so glitter in its eyes, and the answer will be with the prophet, " All flesh is grass, and all the goodliness thereof as the flower of the field," Isa. xl. 6. " Vanity of vanities, all is vanity," Eccl. i. 2. The afflicted soul saith of all creature-excellency, " It is not," Prov. xxiii. 5. it looks upon them as so many nonentities ; so many *nots*. *Not* that which it seems ; *not* that which it promiseth ; *not* that which we expect, and flatter ourselves with. " Riches profit not in the day of wrath," Prov. xi. 4. Whatsoever it is that a man makes his riches, whether friend, or wealth, or parts, or creature-interest, they profit not, that is, they cannot deliver out of the hands, either of death or judgment. And besides, the soul finds by experience the unsuitableness and dissatisfaction that is in all these seen things; that there is no proportion between an invisible soul and visible comforts, between an immortal soul and perishing contentments, between a spiritual being and an earthly portion ; that the wind which a man takes in by gaping will as soon fill an hungry belly, as creature-comforts will satisfy the spirit. In the hour of temptation the soul says, "Miserable comforters are ye all, physicians of no value;" upon which a man may bestow all that he hath in expectation of a cure, as the afflicted woman upon her physicians, Mark v. 26. and find himself no whit better, but rather worse. Surely the world in all its bravery is to the afflicted soul no better than the cities which Solomon gave to Hiram, which he called Cabul, that is to say, displeasing or dirty, 1 Kings ix. 13. The day of affliction is one of those days, wherein men cast away their idols of silver and their idols of gold, which they made each one for himself to worship, to the moles and to the bats, and saith unto them with indignation, Get ye hence, Isa. ii. 20.

Third. In the day of affliction, God discovers to the soul the fulness of Jesus Christ.

There is an infinite fulness in Jesus Christ. "It pleased the Father that in him should all fulness dwell," Col. i. 19. The covenant of grace is suited to all the exigences and indigences of a poor, undone, convinced sinner; it is "ordered in all things," 2 Sam. xxiii. 5. In opposition to the power of corruption in the heart, "I will put," saith God, "my law in their inward parts," &c. Jer. xxxi. 33, 34. In opposition to error and ignorance in the understanding, "They shall all know me," &c. In opposition to guilt, "I will forgive their iniquity, and I will remember their sin no more." And the offices of Jesus Christ are suited to all the branches of the covenant. In order to the first branch, "I will write my law in their hearts," &c. Behold Jesus Christ is a King. In order to the second. "They shall all know me," &c. behold Jesus Christ is a Prophet. And in order to the third, "I will forgive

their iniquities," behold Jesus Christ is a Priest.
The offices of Christ fill and execute the covenant
of grace; and the fulness of God fills and acts the
offices of Jesus Christ; the power of God, and the
fulness of power, his kingly office. The wisdom
of God, and the fulness of wisdom, his prophetical
office. The righteousness of God, and the fulness
of righteousness, his priestly office. This is that
which the psalmist celebrateth in that song of
loves, " God hath anointed thee with the oil of
gladness above thy fellows," Psa. xlv. 7. Never
king was anointed with such power, never prophet with such wisdom, never priest with such
grace and righteousness: they had their stinted proportions; but " God gave not the Spirit by measure
unto him," John iii. 34. " In him dwelt all the
fulness of the Godhead bodily," Col. ii. 9. It is
not less than an infinite fulness which fills Jesus
Christ as Mediator, that we of his fulness might
receive grace for grace. But we are not always in
a capacity either to receive or to see that fulness.
And the reason is, because in our prosperity we *fill*
ourselves so with the world, with the pleasures and
profits of the world, that it fares with Christ now
as it did when he was born, there is no room for
him in the inn. While the world glitters in our eyes
with her painted gaudery, " he hath no form nor
comeliness, and when we see him, there is no beauty
that we should desire him," Isa. liii. 2. We are
very prone to love the world for the world, terminate
our affections in the creature, and do not use
earthly comforts in that way, and to that end, that
we might thereby be the more fitted to walk with
God; and when our desires are such, the more they
are, the less are our delights in Jesus Christ. This

is our sin and folly, that we do not fear the unlawful use of lawful things ; nor see where the
snare lieth to inveigle those affections to the creature which are only due to God himself; and a
great reproach it is to Jesus Christ. But now
when God spreads sackcloth upon all the beauty
and bravery of the creature, and so hideth pride
from man, when God by some flashes of lightning
strikes us blind to the world, then we can discover
beauty and excellency in Christ, infinitely tran-
scending all the beauty and excellency in the world ;
" Thou art fairer than the children of men, grace
is poured into thy lips," Psa. xlv. 2. when under
the stairs, and in the clifts of the rocks, then the
soul can sing, " My beloved is white and ruddy,
the chiefest among ten thousand," Sol. Song, v. 10.
When the God of heaven hath famished all our
gods on earth, when he hath hunger-starved us, as
to creature-comforts, in any way whatsoever, then
we can hunger after and taste the sweetness, the
fulness, which is in Jesus Christ ; O then, Christ, a
King to govern, a Prophet to teach, a Priest to save !
how precious ! then none but Christ, none but
Christ ; give me Christ or else I die. In a word,
my beloved, when once it is come (by what exigences and surprises soever) to an, Oh wretch that
I am, who shall deliver me ? then, " I thank God
through Jesus Christ our Lord," Rom. vii. 24, 25.
Truly God sees it absolutely necessary to exercise
us with a severe discipline, that he may endear
Jesus Christ to our hearts ; and seclude us from
the world, that we may study and improve his
fulness. As the law is our schoolmaster, so affliction
is an usher to the law ; affliction brings us to the
law, and the law brings us to Christ, Gal. iii. 24.

And thus I have despatched the first thing I undertook, for the opening of the doctrine, namely, the lessons which God teacheth those whom he chasteneth; both in their twenty particulars, and in their three summary comprehensive heads, to which all the rest may be reduced.

II. The nature or properties of Divine teaching.

My brethren, it is not every teaching that will make or evidence a man to be a blessed man under affliction. There is hardly any man that is under affliction, but he learns somewhat by it; and yet few are blessed: the reason is, because it matters not so much, what a man is taught, as who is the teacher, whether he be taught of God or not: yea that is not all neither; for we are not to inquire only, whether we be taught of God, but how? There is a twofold teaching of God. There is a common teaching, which even heathen, men out of the church, hypocrites and reprobates within the church, may have; the very philosophers have read excellent lectures upon affliction, Seneca and others; and there is a special teaching, proper and peculiar only to the children of promise   A covenant teaching; " All thy children shall be taught of God," Isa. liv. 13. it is the covenant of God with the Redeemer.   A teaching without which no profit; " I am the Lord thy God which teacheth thee to profit;" to profit by chastisements and correction; so it followeth, " Which leadeth thee by the way that thou shouldest go," Isa. xlviii. 17. God's teachings are not only directing teachings, but leading teachings; not only to show the way, but to enable to go in the way.

Now this teaching hath a six-fold property.

1. It is an inward teaching. Inward in respect of the *object*, and inward in respect of the *subject*.

Inward in respect of the *object;* so our Saviour concerning the saving teaching of the Holy Ghost; " When the Spirit of truth is come, he will guide you into all truth," John xvi. 13. Man may lead you *unto* truth; but it is the Spirit of God that only can lead you *into* truth. He only that hath the key of David, that openeth and no man shutteth, and shutteth and no man openeth, can open to you the door of truth, and show you the inside of truth. And great is the difference between these two teachings. He that comes to a stately house or place sees only the outward fabric and structure; and even that may take much; but he that comes into it, sees all the inward contrivances and conveyances; he sees all the rich furniture and adornings of the several rooms and offices of the house, which are not only for use, but for delight and ornament. Surely, the very outside of truth is goodly; but, like the king's daughter, it is all glorious within; not pleasing only, but ravishing; this they see who are led into truth; by virtue whereof David saw wonderful things in the law, Psa. cxix. 18. Objects which filled his soul with wonder and delight.

As the teachings of the covenant are inward in respect of the object, so inward also in respect of the *subject*. " In the *hidden part* thou hast made me know wisdom," Psa. li. 6. and again, " I thank the Lord that gave me counsel, *my reins* also instruct me in the night seasons," Psa. xvi. 7. The reins are the most inward part of the body; and the night season the most retired and private time;

both express the intimacy of Divine teaching; man may teach the brains, but God only teacheth the reins; the knowledge which man teacheth is a swimming knowledge, but the knowledge which Christ teacheth is a soaking knowledge. " God who commanded light to shine out of darkness, hath shined into our hearts, to give the light of the knowledge of the glory of God in the face of Jesus Christ," 2 Cor. iv. 6. It is a loaden expression, and holds forth the inward teachings of God on both sides; both in reference to the subject, and in reference to the object. In reference to the subject, he that commanded the light to shine out of darkness, hath shined into our hearts; man's light may shine into the head, but God's light doth shine into the heart. God hath his throne in heaven, but his chair, his pulpit, is in the heart; he " hath shined into our hearts." And then you have the inwardness of Divine teaching in respect of the object; " He hath given us the light of the knowledge of the glory of God in the face of Jesus Christ." Man may give knowledge, confused general knowledge, but God giveth the light of knowledge in the lustre and brightness of it. " In thy light we shall see light," Psa. xxxvi. 9. The soul seeth by the same light whereby God himself seeth, "thy light." And not only so; here is not only knowledge and light of knowledge, but the glory of that light; the light which God brings in to the sanctified understanding, is a glorious light, a marvellous light, 1 Pet. ii. 9. The soul that the Spirit of God taketh by the hand, and leadeth into truth, standeth wondering at the glory and excellency of that light which shines round about it. And then lastly, all this in the face of Jesus Christ; the face is the full discovery of a person. Moses could not see God's face, but only his back-parts he might see, Exod. xxxiii. 23. But now by the flesh of Jesus Christ God hath put a vail upon his face; the vail of his flesh, Heb. x. 20. through which we may see the face of God; for now in Christ it is God manifest in the flesh, 1 Tim. iii. 16. the human nature of Jesus Christ hath made God visible. In this face now of Jesus Christ do they whom God teacheth by a saving gospel-teaching see Divine truth, that is, they see it now not only by borrowed representations and natural resemblances, but in its own native beauty and lustre, "as the truth is in Jesus," Eph. iv. 21. "He hath shined into our hearts to give us the light of the knowledge of the glory of God in the face of Jesus Christ." This is the first property of Divine teaching. It is inward, and that both in respect of subject and object.

2. Divine covenant-teaching is a clear convincing teaching; so our Saviour of the Spirit; " When he is come, he shall *convince* the world," &c. The word signifieth a clear demonstrative conviction ; so the apostle defines faith to be the evidence, or demonstration, the evident demonstration of things not seen. The Holy Ghost in his teachings, brings in divine truths with such a clear and convincing light that the soul sits down under it fully satisfied ; it is not only convinced to silence, but to assurance ; the soul doth sweetly and freely acquiesce in the present truths. " Now I know," saith Moses's father-in-law, " that the Lord is greater than all gods." He had heard of God before, but that bred but opinion only ; but now he is thoroughly convinced; " I know that the Lord is greater than all gods," Exod. xviii. 11. So David concerning his afflictions,

" I know, Lord, that thy judgments are right, and that of faithfulness thou hast afflicted me," Psa. cxix. 75. He was fully satisfied both of the equity and fidelity of God's chastisements; right in respect of the merit, and faithful in respect of the end. And thus in all the lessons before presented to your view, and in all other, what God teacheth he teacheth with such a clear evidence of truth, that the soul is set beyond all peradventure; " Our gospel came unto you, not in word only, but also in power and in the Holy Ghost, and in much full assurance," 1 Thess. i. 5. the word hath a double and a treble emphasis; assurance, full assurance, and much full assurance; such are the teachings of the Holy Ghost. Common teaching may convince to silence, a man cannot tell how to gainsay or contradict, but the understanding may remain doubtful still : there is that which the schools call suspense or hesitancy in the understanding ; there is not a full and clear assent in the understanding to the truths propounded : but a man remains, in the apostle's language, a double-minded man : or as the word signifieth, a double-soul man ; a man of a double, or doubtful, or divided spirit, floating between different opinions ; one soul, as it were, believeth this way, and another soul believeth that way ; one while he believeth there is a God, and anon " the fool saith in his heart, There is no God :" sometimes he calls sin evil ; and anon again he thinks it good. He believeth, and he believeth not ; sometimes what he heareth from the word is truth of God ; sometimes he thinks again it is but an invention of man, there may possibly be some mistake in it. But now the teachings of God set a man beyond all those fluctuations and unsettledness

in judgment : there is that which the apostle calls
" the riches of the full assurance of understanding
to the acknowledgment of the mystery of God," Col.
ii. 2.   Assurance of principles, even when the soul
may possibly want the assurance of application.

3. Another property of Divine teaching is, it is
an experimental teaching. The soul can speak
experimentally of the truths it knows, " It is good
for me," saith David, "that I have been afflicted,"
Psa. cxix. 71. why, but may not any man say as
much as that?   Yes, few men there are but have
the notion in their heads, and on their lips : but
mark, I pray, the psalmist speaks experimentally to
the point, and doth instance the good which he had
gained by affliction ; " I have learned thy statutes."
He had learned more acquaintance with the word,
more delight in the word, more conformity to the
word.   He knew it more, and loved it better, and
was more transformed into the nature of it than
ever, &c.   So, " The Lord preserveth the simple,"
Psa. cxvi. 6. that is, God stands by his upright
hearted ones to secure them from violence : a good
notion ; but any man may have it in the proposi-
tion ; but David hath it in the *experience*, " I was
brought low, and he helped me ;" my faith was
brought low, and my comfort was brought low,
and my resolutions were brought low, " my feet had
well nigh slipped," Psa. lxxiii. 2. but God helped my
faith, revived my comfort, strengthened my resolutions, and established my feet : " Thou hast holden
me by my right hand," ver. 23.   Thus St. Paul,
" I know whom I have believed," &c. 2 Tim. i. 12.
I have experienced his faithfulness and his all-suffi--
ciency : I dare trust my all with him.   I am sure
he will keep it safe to that day.   And thus they

that are taught of God in affliction can speak experimentally, in one degree or other, of the gains and privileges of a suffering condition : they can speak experimentally of communion with God, "Though I walk through the valley of the shadow of death, I will fear no evil ;" why? "for thou art with me," Psa. xxiii. 4. I have had comfortable experience of thy upholding, counselling, comforting presence with me in my deepest desertion : so of other fruits of affliction, "This I had," Psa. cxix. 56. this I have got by my sufferings, I bless God I have learned more patience, humility, self-denial, &c. to be more sensible of my brethren's sufferings, to sit looser to the world, to mind duty, and to trust safely with God, to prepare for death, and to provide for eternity, one way or other it is good for me; I could not have been without this affliction, &c.

Common knowledge rests in generals, and lieth more in propositions than in application ; but they that are taught of God can say, As we have heard, so have we *seen;* they can go along with every truth, and say, It is so, I have experienced this word upon mine own heart; they can set to their seal that God is true, John iii. 33.

4. Divine covenant-teaching is a powerful teaching. After a man hath got many truths into the understanding, the main work is yet to do, and that is to bring down holy truths to action, to draw forth Divine principles into practice : a natural man may know much, he may have a heap of truths in his understanding; but they all lie strengthless in the brain, he hath no power to live the truths he knows. Covenant-teachings convey strength as well as light, and do what they teach. "The Lord spake to me with a strong hand, and instructed me that I should

not walk in the way of this people, saying, Say ye not, A confederacy to them who say, A confederacy; neither fear ye their fear, nor be afraid. Sanctify the Lord of hosts himself," &c. Isa. viii. 11—13. It is a most sweet and comfortable scripture, and that in two respects. 1. In respect of what it implieth. 2. In respect of what it expresseth. First, it implieth thus much, that even the holy prophet himself had no small combat and conflict within himself what to do in such a juncture of time as that was, when it was told the house of David, saying, " Syria is confederate with Ephraim," Isa. vii. 2. that is, that both those kingdoms had made a league together, and were now upon their march with their combined forces, to make war against the house of David. It was sad news, and the text saith, " The heart of Ahaz, and the heart of the people was moved, as the trees of the wood are moved with the wind," that is, they were terribly afraid, even ready to die for fear, and in that fear abundance of the people fell off to the enemy, and engaged with them ; as it is intimated, " They refuse the waters of Shiloah that go softly," Isa. viii. 6. that is, they looked upon the forces of Jerusalem, as poor and inconsiderable, no ways able to oppose and engage so potent an adversary as came against them ; and so deserted their own party, and rejoiced in Rezin and Remaliah's son : they rejoiced in them, that is, to cover their defection from their true sovereign they cried up the invaders as their best friends, who came to rescue them from the tyranny and oppression of Ahaz. And it seems the prophet Isaiah himself was surprised with fear too, for a time, and began to dispute the matter within himself, whether it were not best for him, to strike in with the stronger side, and to engage in the confederacy with those two princes as the multitude did; there wanting not, probably, fair and specious pretences to justify that defection. It seems, I say, that the prophet had a sore temptation upon his spirit about this matter, and was even ready to determine the question in the affirmative, till God came in and instructed him, &c. And that is the second thing; the comfort expressed in these words: while the prophet was thus conflicting and fluctuating in his own thoughts, God came in, and by strength of hand rebuked his fears, silenced his objections, quieted his spirit, determined the dispute, and instructed him what course to take, which was not to comply, but to believe, to study duty, and leave safety with God; "Fear not their fear, nor be afraid, sanctify the Lord of hosts himself," &c. Power went forth with instruction, taught him what to do, and enabled him to do what it taught. Blessed be God, who hath a hand to teach his people with, as well as a mouth; a hand of power, as well as a mouth of instruction: had it not been for this, the prophet himself had been certainly carried down the torrent of that apostasy, as well as others.

And there is caution in this instance as well as comfort in reference to ourselves and our brethren; and that is, in case of surprise by some sudden gusts of fear and temptation, not rashly to judge ourselves, or our brethren; but wisely and calmly to consider it is no other temptation than what is common to man, 1 Cor. x. 13. yea to the best of men: Job, and David, and Jeremiah, and Habakkuk, and Peter, and here Isaiah, were all nonplussed, and staggered for a time, and recovered only by a powerful word from Heaven; and therefore in such cases, it becomes christians to pity, rather than to insult, and to study to heal rather than to reject: "Considering themselves, lest they also be tempted," Gal. vi. 1. This is the privilege of the children of promise, strength goeth out from the covenant with instruction, "The Lord who commandeth light to shine out of darkness, hath shined into our hearts:" which means, God had taught us by such a word, as that whereby he made the world, a creating word, a word that giveth strength as well as counsel. And this teaching it is which the prophet David so frequently importuneth in his prayers: compare Psa. cxix. 33. with verse 35. "Teach me, O Lord, the way of thy statutes, make me to go in the path of thy commandments." "Teach me to do thy will," Psa. cxliii. 10. Mark that; not only teach me *the way*, but teach me *to go;* not only teach me thy will, but teach me to do thy will. Common teaching may teach a hypocrite the way, but having teaching only teacheth the soul *to go* in that way; an unregenerate man may know the will of God; but he knoweth not how to *do* that will. "The joy of the Lord is our strength," Neh. viii. 10.

5. A fifth property; the teachings of God are sweet and pleasant teachings. "Thou hast taught me;" what followeth? "How sweet are thy words unto my taste! yea sweeter than honey to my mouth." Psa. cxix. 102, 103. He rolled the word and promises as sugar under his tongue, and sucked from thence more sweetness than Samson did from his honey-comb. Luther said, he would not live in paradise, if he must live without the word; but with the word, saith he, I could live in hell itself. When Christ puts in his teaching hand by the hole of the door to teach the heart, "his fingers drop

sweet smelling myrrh upon the handles of the lock," Sol. Song v. 5. The teachings of Christ leave a sweet remembrance of himself behind them; 'We will remember thy love more than wine," Sol. Song i. 4. As people, when they drink wine, are apt to sing; so those that are filled with the Spirit, cannot but triumph in the wonderful things which they taste and see in the word. There cannot be but much spiritual joy in Divine teaching, because the Spirit doth accompany the truths, and so irradiate them with his own beauty and glory, the light of the knowledge of the glory of God in the face of Christ, that they do not only affect, but ravish the heart: "Thy word is pure, therefore thy servant loveth it," Psa. cxix. 140. The prophet saw a beam of Divine excellency sitting upon the word, and that did happily ensnare his soul. Truth is burdensome to unsound spirits, because convincing; and they labour to extinguish that light which disturbeth their quiet: "They hold the truth in unrighteousness," Rom. i. 18. in the Septuagint, They imprison the truth, and will not suffer it to do its office. But saving teaching is sweet and delightful, because it is suitable to the renewed part; to which it comes in with fresh succours, to relieve and fortify it against the assaults of opposite corruption: I say, it is always sweet in that respect, but never more sweet than in affliction; the bitterness of adversity giving a more delicate relish unto the word, by healing the distempers of the spiritual palate: and then the soul crieth out with Jeremiah in the prison, "Thy words were found, and I did eat them, and thy word was unto me the joy and the rejoicing of my heart," Jer. xv. 16.

6. Divine teaching is an abiding teaching: "The

anointing which ye have received of him abideth in you," 1 John ii. 27. Notional knowledge, where it is no more, is flitting and inconsistent, and leaveth the soul dubious and uncertain. Observe how the apostle James expresseth it, speaking of the mere notional hearer, "He beholdeth himself, and goeth his way, and straightway forgetteth what manner of man he was," James i. 24. Observe, he doth not only forget what he heard, but he forgets what he was. The glass, whether word or affliction, discovered to him his spots, showed him his pride, his covetousness, the impurity of heart and life, &c. but he goeth away, and forgetteth what manner of man he was ; he forgets the word, he forgets the rod, and what both word and rod discovered to him, together with the resolutions and promises made to God in both. A godly man may forget the word, a gracious heart may have a bad memory ; but he will not so easily forget himself, he doth not forget his spots, and that keeps him in continual work, to wash and purge himself from all filthiness of flesh and spirit " Remembering mine affliction and my misery, the wormwood and the gall. My soul hath them still in remembrance, and is humbled in me," Lam. iii. 19, 20. "The double-minded man is unstable in all his ways," James i. 8. Human teaching begets at best but opinion, not faith ; the word implieth one that is distracted and divided in his thoughts, floating betwixt two contrary opinions. There are notions contradicting notions, and principles fighting against principles ; and such knowledge is not abiding knowledge: this unfixedness in principles produceth instability in practice. If a man be double-minded in his principles, he will be unstable in all his ways : none are so constant in the profession of any truth, as they that are fully convinced and assured of it : none so stable in their conversation, as they that are rooted and established in the present truth. This is the effect of God's teaching, it keeps the judgment steady, and the heart stable.

"Teach me, O Lord, the way of thy statutes, and I will keep it unto the end," Psa. cxix. 33. He dares promise perseverance, if God will undertake instruction : and accordingly he made good his promise, upon this very account ; "I have not departed from thy judgments, for thou hast taught me." Observe it ; he doth not say, I will keep thy statutes ; but he can say, and that many years after, " I have kept thy statutes." Many will say in their affliction, I will keep thy statutes ; promise fair, if God will but deliver them : but how few can say with David, " I have kept, I have not departed from thy judgments !" "Of old time," saith God, " I have broken thy yoke, and burst thy bonds, and thou saidst, I *will not* transgress ; when upon every high hill, and under every green tree thou wanderest, playing the harlot," Jer. ii. 20. Good words in trouble, but poor performance out of trouble : no sooner out of affliction, but they fall again to their old trade of spiritual adultery against God : no sooner their old hearts and their old temptations meet, but they close, and embrace one another ; they started aside like a broken bow. But David was taught of God, and therefore he is as careful to make good his vows as to make good vows; " I will pay thee my vows, which my lips have uttered, and my mouth hath spoken, when I was in trouble," Psa.lxvi. 13, 14. The after part of David's life was much more severe and exact than the former : " I have not departed from thy judgments, for thou hast taught me."

These are the properties of Divine teachings: but lest I should lay a snare before the blind, and make the heart sad, which God would not have made sad; I must of necessity lay in a few brief cautions.

When we say God teacheth inwardly, clearly, experimentally, powerfully, sweetly, abidingly, our meaning is not so to be understood, as if God taught all at first; namely, either all truths, or all of any truth. God doth not teach all his lessons at the first entrance into the school of affliction; at least not usually, for we dare not limit God. The fruit of affliction is not gathered presently: " No chastening for the present seemeth to be joyous, but grievous nevertheless afterward it yieldeth the peaceable fruits of righteousness unto them which are exercised thereby," Heb. xii. 11. Teaching is the fruit of affliction, and fruit is not gathered presently; it must have a ripening time. And therefore, O thou discouraged soul, say not God doth not teach thee at all, if he do not teach thee all at once. "The entrance of thy word giveth light." God lets in light by degrees: usually God teacheth his children, as we teach ours, now a little, and then a little, Isa. xxviii. 10. somewhat this week, and more next week; somewhat by this affliction, and more by the next affliction, and more by a third, &c. It is not to be despised if God discover to the soul the need of Divine teaching, and engage the heart in holy desires, and longings after it; so that the afflicted soul can say in sincerity, " My soul breaketh for the longing that it hath unto thy judgments at all times," Psa. cxix. 20.

When we say, that God teacheth whom he chasteneth, and teacheth them thus and thus; it is not to be understood as if he taught all alike. God hath several forms in the school of affliction, as well as in the school of the word. There are fathers for experience, young men for strength, and babes for the truth and being of grace, 1 John ii. 12. And, therefore, if God have not taught thee so much as another, say not. He hath not taught me at all. As one star differeth from another in glory, so also is the school of Christ. It is free grace thou art a star, though thou art not a star of the first or second magnitude; that God hath let in some Divine light, though not so much light as another may possibly have; that thou art in God's school, though, it may be, not in the highest form. In point of holy emulation we should look at the degrees of grace; but in point of thankfulness and comfort we should look at the truth and being of grace.

When we say that God teacheth powerfully and abidingly, it is not to be understood as if these teachings did put the soul into an immutable evenness of spirit, or freed it from all insurrections and disturbances from opposite corruption. Such a frame of soul is only the privilege of the glorified estate, wherein we shall see God face to face, and dwell in immutability itself to all eternity. Here the church hath its fulls and its wains. David had his sinkings, and Job his impatient fits; we have heard of the patience of Job, yea and of his impatience too: moved the taught of God may be, but not removed; fall they may, but not fall away; fearfully, but not finally; terribly, but not totally.

But these things are inseparable to covenant teaching.

(1.) The soul is thereby made sensible of the

least stirrings and whisperings of corruption. I find a law in my members warring against the law of my mind, Rom. vii. 23. Others have it, but they do not *find* it, .they are not sensible of the law in their members, &c.

(2.) They are exceedingly displeased with the opposition they find in their natures against the teachings of God; and do rise up in indignation against all that contradiction which is in the unregenerate part, in what kind soever. " Why art thou cast down, O my soul? and why art thou so disquieted within me?" Is there cause for this despondency? is this done like a David, like a man after God's own heart? Is this the fruit of all the experiences of God's faithfulness and all-sufficiency? and so in other cases doth the soul chide down distempers, and uncomely workings of spirit: the soul is full of displicence* against itself; " So foolish was I, and ignorant: I was as a beast before thee," Psa. lxxiii. 22. it cannot find words bad enough to give itself.

(3.) And if that will not do, then they go to God in prayer, and spread their temptations before the Lord; " O my God, my soul is cast down within me," Psa. xlvi. 6. When they cannot lay the storm, and still the tempests by their own word, then, with the disciples in the ship, they go and awaken Christ, and desire him by his powerful word to rebuke them, that there may be a calm. They go and pray out their distempers, and pray their hearts into a better frame: as once it was said of Luther, that when he found distempers upon his spirit, he would never give over praying, till he had prayed his heart into that frame he prayed for.

* Discontent, dislike

(4) By virtue of the teachings of God they are enabled to maintain opposition against all the evil which they find in their own spirits. " As the flesh lusteth against the spirit, so the spirit lusteth against the flesh," Gal. v. 17. that is, the spiritual regenerate part doth as naturally rise up and make war against the flesh, and fleshly motions, as the flesh doth against the teachings of God in the spiritual part. Opposition is not only maintained by precept and rules, and an extrinsical policy, but naturally, and by virtue of an inward antipathy ; the spirit lusteth. The spiritual opposition is as suitable and agreeable to the new nature, as the sinful opposition is to the old nature. Hence is the life of a believer called a wrestling, a warfare, Eph. vi. 12.

(5.) Not only so, but by the help of Divine teaching the soul gets ground of that fleshly opposition, wherewith it is molested, by degrees. " In the day when I cried, thou answeredst me ; and strengthenedst me with strength in my soul," Psa. cxxxviii. 3. Prayer brought in God, and God brought in strength, whereby he got ground of his distempers ; and though all was not done at first, yet his comfort was, all should be done in God's time, " The Lord will perfect that which concerneth me," ver. 8. I am not perfect, but I shall be perfected. " He that hath begun a good work, will perform it till the day of Jesus Christ," Phil. i. 6.

(6.) Though the soul be not always the same for temper and acting, yet it is always the same for purpose and design. " Then shall I not be ashamed, when I have respect unto all thy commandments." Though he could not *keep* all, he could *respect* all the commandments of God. " My soul followeth hard after God," Psa. lxiii. 8. Clouds of opposition intercepted and disturbed his sweet and constant communion with God sometimes; but he brake through that crowd by main strength to recover God's presence again; " My soul followeth hard after thee;" and Paul is pressing after perfection when he could not overtake it, Phil. iii. 12, 13.

(7.) The soul hath not always, possibly, the same *relish* and taste of Divine truths and ordinances, but it hath the same *estimate*, it keeps up high appreciating thoughts of spiritual things ; and when it cannot relish them, yet even then it doth *hunger* after them. " My soul breaketh for the longings it hath unto thy judgments *at all times*," Psa. cxix. 20. And the promise is made to hunger, &c. Matt. v. 6.

And yet, even in reference to these dispositions, which I call inseparable concomitants to saving teaching, I must add this one caution in close of all ; namely, that allowance be made in case of desertion. A child of God, for causes which here we cannot stand to mention, may be cast into so deep a state of desertion, for a time, that he may, as the apostle speaks, " forget that he was purged from his old sins," 2 Pet. i. 9. " A child of light may walk in darkness," Isa. l. 10. And though there be no such swoon in the new man, wherein both habits and acts do cease, yet they may be so stupified by the impressions of the present temptation, as the poor soul shall be sensible of neither, but reduced into such a state as that there may be life, but no sense of that life.

Thus much therefore for the second thing propounded in the doctrinal part; the nature and properties of Divine teaching. I come now to,

III. The third thing propounded, namely, to inquire, How affliction lieth in order to instruction? what tendency chastisement hath to promote the teachings of God in the soul? what use God makes of correction to this end?

For it may possibly be demanded, Might not God as well teach his people by sin as by affliction? He might, and doth: whence that gloss of Augustine upon Rom. viii. 28. " All things work together for good to them that love God," even sin itself; and inasmuch as he saith "all things," it is evident he excepteth nothing, that doth not co-operate for good to the called according to God's purpose. All things *do work*, but all things do not work *alike*. Sin works for good, but it is by absolute omnipotence, by pure prerogative; for sin is properly the devil's creature, and in its own natural tendency works merely to destruction; no thanks to sin that any good comes of it; God beats Satan with his own weapons. But affliction is an evil of *God's making*, as Amos iii. 6. and he hath so tempered the nature of it, and doth so ingredient it by his Divine skill, that there is some fitness and disposition in it to serve and promote his own gracious designs in the children of promise. It is true, there is need of an arm of Omnipotence to make chastisement to have a saving influence upon the heart; and so there doth also even in the word itself, and Divine ordinances; they do not save by any intrinsical virtue, or power of their own; but yet there is a passive fitness in them to serve Omnipotence for Divine and saving ends; a fitness of instrumentality, Heb. iv. 12. as there is in a saw to cut, and in a wedge to cleave, &c. The instrument can do nothing alone, but there is a fitness in it to serve the hand of the workman. And thus it is, in a proportion, with affliction; it is true, there is not so immediate and direct a tendency in the rod, as there is in the word, to teach and instruct the children of God; yet there is in chastisement a subserviency to prepare the heart of man, and to put it into a better disposition to close with Divine teaching, than naturally it is capable of. The hot furnace is Christ's workhouse, the most excellent vessels of honour are formed therein. Manasseh, Paul, the jailer, were all chosen in this fire; as God saith, "I have chosen thee in the furnace of affliction," Isa. xlviii. 10. Grace works in a powerful, yet in a moral way. God speaks when we are most apt to hear; congruously, yet forcibly, by a fit accommodation of circumstances; which you may discover in these four particulars:

1. By correction God taketh down the pride of man's heart. There is not a greater obstruction to saving knowledge than pride and self-opinion, whereby man either thinks he knoweth enough, or, that not worth the learning which God teacheth; therefore it is proclaimed before the word, " Hear and give ear, be not proud; for the Lord hath spoken," Jer. xiii. 15. In Divine matters, as well as human, " only by pride cometh contention," Prov. xiii. 10. It is pride which raiseth objections against the word, and disputeth the commands when it should obey them. The proud men in Jeremiah, Jer. xliii. 2. when they could elude tho message of God by his prophet no longer, do at length stiffen into downright rebellion: first they shift, " Thou speakest falsely," &c. ver. 2. and then

they resolve, " As for the word that thou hast spoken to us in the name of the Lord, we will not hearken unto thee," &c. Jer. xliv. 16. which means, Be it Baruch, or be it God, we will have none of it ; " but we will certainly do whatsoever goeth forth out of our own mouth," &c. Such a master-piece of obduration is the heart of man, that it stands like a mountain before the word, and cannot be moved, till *God* come with his instruments of affliction, and digging down those mountains (as it is proclaimed before the gospel, Luke iii. 5.) casteth them into a level ; and then God may stand, as it were, upon even ground, and talk with man. This pride of heart speaketh loud in the wicked, and whispereth too audibly even in the godly ; it is a folly bound up even in the hearts of God's children, till the correction driveth it out ; and the proud stomach being broken, the poor bleeding wretch cries out, " Lord, what wilt thou have me to do ?"

2. Affliction is God's forge wherein he softens the iron heart. There is no dealing with the iron while it remaineth in its own native coldness and hardness ; put it into the fire, make it red hot there, and you may stamp upon it any figure or impression you please. " God maketh my heart soft." saith Job, Job xxiii. 16. Melted vessels are impressive to any form. So it is with the heart of man ; naturally it is colder and harder than the northern iron ; and that native induration is much increased by prosperity, and the patience of God towards sinners ; the iron sinew will rather break than bend. It is the hot furnace only which can make it operable and impressive to God's counsels : which course therefore, God resolveth on ; " I will melt them and try them," Jer. ix. 7. and sometimes God

is forced to make the furnace seven times hotter, to work out that dross which renders men so unformable to the ministry of the word, while God sends his prophets, rising up early, and sending them; and yet they will not incline their ear, but harden their necks against Divine instruction.

When the earthly heart of a man is so dried and hardened by a long sunshine of prosperity, that the plough of the spiritual husbandman cannot enter, God doth soften it with showers of adversity, maketh it capable of the immortal seed, and blesseth the springing thereof, Psa. lxv. 10. The seed falleth upon stony ground, till God turn the stone into a heart of flesh.

3. By chastisement man is made more attentive unto God. In prosperity the world makes such a noise in a man's ears, that God cannot be heard; he speaks indeed once and twice, again and again, very often; "yet man perceiveth it not," Job xxxiii. 14. he is so busy in the crowd of worldly affairs, that God is not heeded. In the godly themselves there is much unsettledness and giddiness of mind; naturally our thoughts are vain and scattered, the spirit slippery and inconsistent, which is a great impediment to our clear and full comprehensions of spiritual things. And therefore God deals with man as a father with his child playing in the market-place, and will not hear or mind his father's call; he comes and takes him out of the noise of the tumult, carries him into his house, lays him upon his knee with the rod in his hand, and then the father can be heard: so doth God, I say, with his children. "He openeth their ears," Job xxxiii. 16. Hebrew. He uncovereth their ears, which the world had stopped, and then instruction will

enter. When Joab would not come to Absalom, he sets his field on fire, 2 Sam. xiv. 30. And thus after neglects God brings us to treat with him by affliction. God saith as it were, " Come, let us reason together;" and the soul echos back again, " Speak Lord, for thy servant heareth :" and when the soul is thus silent unto God, he cometh and sealeth instruction by his Spirit.

4. Affliction is an eye-salve, whereby God openeth the eye of the soul to see the need and excellency of Divine teaching, by the discovery of its own brutish ignorance of God, and of his ways, under all Divine administrations. As Ephraim once bemoaned himself to the Lord, "I have been as a bullock, unaccustomed to the yoke." The prophet David will English it, " So foolish was I, and ignorant: I was as a beast before thee," Psa. lxxiii. 22. And by means of this discovery God draws out the heart into humble and holy supplication for Divine teaching ; " That which I see not teach thou me ; and if I have done iniquity, I will do no more," Job xxxiv. 32. When or how cometh the sinner thus to put in for instruction? why, " I have borne chastisement," ver. 31. Correction discovered the need of instruction ; " That which I see not, teach thou me." And thus Ephraim, " Thou hast chastised me, and I was chastised ;" but blows alone will not do it ; therefore it follows, " Turn thou me, and I shall be turned." Though chastisement alone could not turn Ephraim, yet it made him see an absolute necessity of Divine power to his conversion; less than Omnipotence would not serve the turn.

And when God hath brought the heart once into this frame, to see, and be affected with the sense of its own ignorance and impotency, and to lie in the dust at God's feet, humbly importuning an effectual teaching from heaven ; if God should withhold it, he should fail not in his promise only, but his own counsel and project ; in reference to which God cannot lie. But when he hath prepared the heart to pray, he will cause his ear to hear, Psa. x. 17. When God hath engaged the heart in holy desires of saving instruction, it is not mercy only in God, but faithfulness, to satisfy the desire of his own creation. " Good and upright is the Lord, therefore he will teach sinners in the way," Psa. xxv. 8.

IV. The grounds and demonstrations of the point. Of which in a few words, and then I shall come to the use and application.

It must needs be a blessed thing when correction and instruction meet, if we consider—

1. The lessons themselves which God teacheth his Ephraims in the school of affliction. For in-stance, is it not a blessed thing to be taught how to compassionate them that are in a suffering con-dition ? yea, saith the psalmist, " Blessed is he that considereth the poor, the Lord will deliver him in time of trouble, the Lord will preserve him, and keep him alive, and he shall be blessed upon earth," Psa. xli. 1, 2. &c. He is blessed, and he shall be blessed, not in heaven only, but upon earth also; and that with a multiplied blessing : see a troop follows ; " Thou wilt not deliver him unto the will of his enemies ; the Lord will strengthen him upon the bed of his languishing ; thou wilt make all his bed in his sickness," ver. 2, 3. Oh the blessedness of a compassionate heart towards afflicted ones! how easy must that bed be which God maketh !

And, is it not a blessed thing to know how to value our earthly comforts without doating upon them? to be thankful, and yet not to surfeit? " Blessed is he that feareth always," that is, who feareth a snare in all his earthly contentments.

And if it be a blessedness to be conformed to Jesus Christ, then surely self-denial is a lesson which will make one blessed. " If any man will come after me, let him deny himself, and take up his cross and follow me," saith our Saviour, Matt. xvi. 24. And, " Blessed are the poor in spirit, for theirs is the kingdom of heaven," and, " Blessed are the meek, for they shall inherit the earth," Matt. v. 3, 5.

If heaven and earth can make one blessed, then humility is a blessed lesson. And so it is, to have our hearts discovered to ourselves; corruption is matter of humiliation, but sight and sense of corruption is matter of comfort and rejoicing. It is a miserable thing indeed to be poor and not to see one's poverty, Thou sayest thou art rich, but knowest not that thou art poor and miserable, Rev. iii. 17. But happy is that man to whom the Lord first discovers the hidden corruption of his heart, and then teacheth him to mourn over it; " Blessed are they that mourn for they shall be comforted," Matt. v. 4.

A man is never in a happier condition than when his heart is in a praying frame. It is a mercy with a note of observation; " Behold he prayeth," Acts ix. 11. a man is never miserable but when he cannot pray.

And, what think ye of the world? surely he is a blessed man that by affliction is brought acquainted with his bible, which is nothing else but a treasury and magazine of blessings: " Blessed is the man whom thou chastisest, O Lord, and teachest him out of thy law." It is your text, and the first psalm is your comment, " His delight is in the law of the Lord, and in his law doth he meditate day and night," ver. 2. And blessed are they whom the Lord teacheth to clear out their evidences for heaven, to give all diligence to make their calling and election sure, for so an abundant entrance shall be administered unto them into the everlasting kingdom of our Lord and Saviour Jesus Christ, 2 Pet. i. 10, 11. When others shall but creep to heaven as it were upon all-fours, they shall ride as in a triumphant chariot into the gates of the new Jerusalem.

Blessed are they, who weep over their grievings of God's Spirit, for God shall wipe off those tears from their eyes; and he will comfort them whom they have grieved. And what is the blessedness of heaven itself, but communion with God! The exercise of grace. The life of faith. Trust in God that raises the dead, and calls things which are not as though they were, and a clearer discovery of God's excellences. What are these but heaven begun on this side heaven, glory antedated! " This is life eternal to know thee," John xvii. 3. our Saviour saith not, it shall be life eternal, but *it is;* eternal life is begun already where these things are.

To be taught the duties and privileges of a suffering condition, is a blessed teaching, for hereby the soul is enabled to taste and see what is good and sweet in every affliction, and is set above all that which is grievous and intolerable to nature; " For this cause we faint not," &c. The one only thing necessary, must necessarily be a blessed thing;　It is," saith our Saviour, " the better part which shall not be taken away," Luke x. 42.

The art of time redemption is a blessing, not less than an evidence of soul redemption ; if ye compare the first epistle of Peter, chap. i. ver. 17 and 18. together.　Ask St. Paul, and he will tell you, that the knowledge of the sufferings of Jesus Christ is an excellent knowledge, in comparison of which all other things are loss and dung, Phil. iii. 8—10.　And to long for heaven is the very first fruits of heaven ; the evidence and seal of our conjugal contract with Jesus Christ ; " The Spirit and the bride say, Come, Lord Jesus," Rev. xxii. 17. 20. Behold christians, to be taught of God when chastised by him, is a blessedness compounded of several precious ingredients ; at least if ye will take in,

2. The nature and properties of Divine teaching ; to be taught all these inwardly, clearly, experimentally, powerfully, sweetly, abidingly.　This must needs be a blessed teaching, it being a teaching which doth possess the soul of the excellences which it discovereth.　Doctrinal and notional knowledge is a blessing; " Blessed," saith Christ to his hearers, " are your eyes, for they see ; and your ears, for they hear," Matt. xiii. 16.　But it is but an occasional, preparatory blessedness, blessedness in the offer and opportunity ; oh but to be taught these lessons with these qualifications ; to be taught the truth as it is in Jesus; to be taught into the nature and image of the truth ; to be taught into the possession of Divine excellences ; this is blessedness indeed ; blessedness in being; full, perfect, fruitional blessedness.

3. A teaching chastisement is the fruit of God's

distinguishing love. Chastisements, simply considered in themselves, lie in common to all the sons and daughters of Adam since the fall; the fruit of that first apostasy, as well as of actual and personal departures from God : yea and deliverance also, lieth in common. Providence dispenseth deliverance to the worst of men. The 106th Psalm is a psalm of promises, made to the church ; but the next psalm, the 107th, is a psalm of providential dispensations to the world ; and there, as you find affliction, so you may find deliverance also out of those afflictions, to be the portion of wicked men ; rebels, ver. 11. and fools, ver. 19, 20. (that is, wicked fools, Solomon's fools all along the Proverbs,) seamen, ver. 23. (for the most part, not the most religious order in the world ;) all these are delivered out of their troubles. The worst of men, I say, share in this fruit of God's providential goodness, deliverance ; but a teaching sanctified affliction is the privy seal of special love, " My *loving kindness* will I not take from him," Psa. lxxxix. 33. " Whom the Lord *loveth* he chasteneth," Heb. xii. 6. that is to say, with a teaching chastisement. When word and rod meet together, when correction and instruction kiss each other, they are the fruit of paternal affection, and therefore must needs have a blessing bound up in them. " As a man chasteneth his son, so the Lord chasteneth thee," Deut. viii. 5.

4. A teaching correction is a branch of the covenant of grace, which God hath made in Christ for the children of promise ; " All thy children shall be taught of God," Isa. liv. 13. " They shall all know me from the least of them, to the greatest," Jer. xxxi. 34. By virtue of Divine teaching affliction is adopted a branch in the covenant of grace. That

89th Psalm is a song of the new covenant; "I will sing of the mercies of the Lord," ver. 1. What mercies? not providence mercies only, but promise mercies, covenant mercies; "I have made a covenant with my chosen," ver. 3. And amongst the rest of the branches of the covenant you shall find the *rod* and the *whip* have their place; "If his children forsake my law, and walk not in my judgments, &c. Then will I visit their transgression with the rod, and their iniquity with stripes," ver. 30—32. Behold rod and stripes standing here, not upon mount Ebal, the mount of curses, as branches of a covenant of works, but upon mount Gerizim, the mount of blessings, Deut. xi. 29. as branches of the covenant of grace. Affliction is not so much threatened as promised to Christ's seed. " My covenant will I not break " Psa. lxxxix. 34. When God seems even to break the bones and hearts of his people by sore and heavy strokes of correction, yet he doth not break his covenant, " My covenant will I not break." It is in order to the covenant when God chastiseth his children, and instructs them by his chastisements. Affliction separated from instruction is pure wrath, a blast from mount Ebal, Deut. xxviii. but by a matrimonial covenant those two scriptures, " I will visit," &c. Psa. lxxxix. 32. and " I will teach," Isa. liv. 13. are married together, and made one spirit, as in my text, and then they are pure grace. The covenant is the Magna Charta of heaven, and contains a list of whatever God the Father hath purposed, God the Son hath purchased, and God the Holy Ghost doth apply to the heirs of promise. The breasts of the covenant run nothing but the milk of spiritual blessing to the children of God.

5. A teaching affliction is the purchase of Christ's death and bloodshed. Christ died not to exempt his redeemed from suffering, but to sanctify their sufferings with his own blood: "I pray not that thou shouldst take them out of the world, but that thou shouldst keep them from the evil," John xvii. 15. Whatsoever Christ purchased, he prayed for; and this was one main privilege, not freedom from the evil of affliction, but from the evil of sin; "Sanctify them through thy truth," ver. 17. God's teachings are sanctifying teachings; "Sanctify them through thy truth: thy word is truth:" Christ's blood purchased nothing but blessings.

6. A teaching affliction is the result of all the offices of Jesus Christ. As a King, he chastens; as a Prophet, he teacheth; and as a Priest, he hath purchased this grace of his Father, that the *rod* might blossom; that *correction* might be consecrated for *instruction* unto the redeemed. Behold, a sanctified affliction is a cup whereinto Jesus Christ hath wrung and pressed the juice and virtue of all his mediatorial offices; surely that must be a cup of generous and royal wine, like that in the supper, a cup of blessing to the people of God.

And thus I have finished the fourth particular propounded for the clearing and confirming of the doctrine, the grounds and demonstrations of the point; and with it the whole doctrinal part of this great and blessed truth, namely, That it is a blessed thing when correction and instruction, word and rod go together.

I come now to the use, for the improvement of the point. And it may serve,

I. For information.

II. For exhortation.

I. For information, and that in these particulars:

1. If they only be blessed whom God chasteneth and teacheth; then affliction alone is not enough to evidence a man to be a happy man. No man is therefore blessed because he is chastened: blows alone are not enough, either to evince or to effect a state of blessedness. "Thou hast chastised me, and I was chastised," Jer. xxxi. 18. crieth repenting Ephraim; which means, I have had blows enough, if blows would have done me good: nay, but under all the strokes and smitings of thy displeasure, I have been as a bullock unaccustomed to the yoke; unteachable and untractable; thou hast drawn one way, and I have drawn another; thou hast pulled forward, and I have pulled backward; all thy chastisements have left me as they found me, brutish and rebellious. Surely blows only may break the neck sooner than the heart. They are in themselves the fruit of Divine wrath, a branch of the curse, and therefore cannot possibly of themselves make the least argument of God's love to the soul. Bastards have blows as well as children, and fools because of their transgression are afflicted, Psa. cvii. 1. And yet it is very sad to consider that this is the best evidence that the most of men have for heaven; because they suffer in this world, they think they shall be freed from sufferings in the world to come; and because they have a hell here, they hope they shall escape hell hereafter, they hope they shall not have *two* hells: yes, poor deluded soul, thou mayest have two hells, and must have two hells without better evidence for heaven. Cain had two hells, and Judas had two hells, and millions of reprobate men and women have two

hells; one of this life, in torments of body, and horror of conscience; and another of the life to come, in unquenchable fire: and so I say shalt thou, unless thou dost get better evidence for heaven, than the present misery which is upon thee. The plagues and evils which are upon thee may be but the beginnings of sorrows: pain now in the body may be but a forerunner of torments hereafter in thy soul: thou mayst have a prison on earth, and a dungeon in hell; thou mayst now want a crumb of bread, and hereafter a drop of water; thou mayst now be the reproach of men, and hereafter the scorn of men and angels, and of God himself. And therefore be wise to salvation, by working it out with fear and trembling, Phil. ii. 12. and giving all diligence, "make your calling and election sure," 2 Pet. i. 10. God forbid that a man should take that for his security from hell, which may be but the prelibations of hell, the pledge and aggravation of endless misery.

Why, but doth not the scripture say, "Whom the Lord loveth he chasteneth, and scourgeth every son whom he receiveth?" Heb. xii. 6. And again, "As many as I love, I rebuke and chasten?" Rev. iii. 19.

Yes: but mark, I beseech you; though the scripture saith, "Whom the Lord loveth he chasteneth," it doth not say, Whomsoever the Lord chasteneth he loveth. Though it saith, "He scourgeth every son whom he receiveth," it doth not say, Whomsoever he scourgeth he receiveth him as a son. Christ saith, "As many as I love, I rebuke and chasten;" but he saith not, As many as I rebuke and chasten, I love. These scriptures include children, but they do not exclude bastards: they tie chastening to sonship, but not sonship to chastening: the sons are chastened; but all the chastened are not, *therefore*, sons: the beloved are rebuked, but all that are rebuked are not, *consequently*, beloved.

But that place in Job v. 17. seems to say as much, " Behold, happy is the man whom God correcteth."

It is true; but one scripture must interpret another; David must expound Eliphaz: " Happy is the man whom God correcteth," that is, when instruction goeth along with correction, when chastisement and teaching accompany one another: " Blessed is the man whom thou chastenest, O Lord, and teachest him out of thy law." The scripture doth not usually give things their names, but when they are made up of all their integrals " Whoso findeth a wife, findeth a good thing, and obtaineth favour of the Lord," Prov. xviii. 22. that is, a wife made up of scripture qualifications: otherwise a man may (and many men do) find a plague in a wife, and hath her from the Lord in wrath, and not in love. Every married woman is not a wife; a bad woman is but the shadow of a wife and so here in this case, &c.

Indeed chastening and affliction is an opportunity of mercy, a may-be to happiness, but not, singly, an evidence of happiness: lay no more upon it than it will bear; it is an opportunity, improve it; it is no more, do not trust it.

2. This doctrine informs us thus much, that as affliction, simply considered, is not enough to make or evidence a man to be happy, so neither is it sufficient to conclude a man to be miserable. No man is therefore miserable because afflicted. It

may prove a teaching affliction, and then he is happy. And yet this is another mistake among men; both in reference to others, and in reference to ourselves. In reference to others; people are very prone to judge them wretched whom they see afflicted: it was the miserable mistake of Job's friends to conclude him miserable because smitten, cursed because chastened. In reference to ourselves; it is a merciless mistake, sometimes even of God's own children, to sit down under affliction, especially if sore and of long continuance, and conclude God doth not love them, because he doth correct them. It seems to be the very case of the believing Hebrews; they judged themselves out of God's favour, because under God's frowns, Heb. xii. not at all beloved, because so greatly afflicted; under many and sore persecutions, as you may see, chap. x. 32—34. And therefore it is that upon which the apostle (after he presented them with a large catalogue and list of the primitive martyrs before Christ, in the eleventh chapter) bestows the twelve first verses of the twelfth chapter, to prove by reasons drawn from nature, and instances taken out of scripture; the first whereof is that unparalleled and astonishing instance of Jesus Christ, the first born, the Son of God's loves and delights. I say, to establish this as a conclusion of unquestionable verity, namely, that God's *love* and God's *rod* may stand together.

The truth is, my brethren, there is nothing can make a man miserable but sin. It is sin that poisons our afflictions: "The sting of death is sin," 1 Cor. xv. 56. and so we may say of all other evils, which militate under death, as soldiers under their general. The sting of sickness is sin; and the sting of poverty is sin; and the sting of imprisonment and banishment is sin: and so of the rest. Take the sting out, which is purchased by the blood of Christ, and evidenced by Divine teaching, and they cannot hurt nor destroy in all God's holy mountain, Isa. xi. 9. And therefore let no children of God be rash to conclude hard things against themselves, and to make evidences of wrath where God hath made none. Let christians on both sides look further than the affliction itself; the Holy Ghost having long since determined this controversy by a peremptory decision: "No man knoweth either love or hatred by all that is before them," Eccl. ix. 1. that is, no man can make a judgment, either of God's love or hatred towards him, by any of these outward dispensations. "He causeth his sun to shine upon the evil, and upon the good; and sendeth rain on the just, and on the unjust," Matt. v. 45. The sun of prosperity shineth upon the dunghill, as well as upon the bed of spices; and the rain of adversity falleth upon the fruitful garden, as well as upon the barren wilderness. He judgeth truly of his estate, that judgeth by the word, and not by providence. Evidences of grace consist in inward impressions, not in outward dispensations.

3. That deliverance out of trouble is not enough to evidence or make a man happy. It is not said, Blessed is the man whom thou chastenest, O Lord, and *deliverest* him out of trouble; but, "Blessed is the man whom thou chastenest and teachest." A man may get rid of the affliction, and yet miss of the blessing. All the bread which men may eat without the sweat of their brows is not therefore hallowed; abundance may flow in without

labour, and yet not without a curse, Gen. iii. 16. A man may leave his chains and his blessing behind him in prison; and the fire of a fever may be extinguished, when the fire of hell is preparing for the sinner. It is good to be thankful for, but extremely dangerous to be contented with, a *bare* deliverance. I shall conclude this branch with this note, which alone might have stood for a distinct observation or corollary—That those prayers in troubles are not best heard which are answered with deliverance; but those prayers are best heard which are answered with instruction. Even of our blessed Saviour it is said, "In the days of his flesh he offered up prayers and supplications with strong crying and tears, unto him that was able to save him from death, and *was heard* in that he feared," Heb. v. 7. How was he heard? not in that, "Save me from this hour," John xii. 27. but in that, " Father, glorify thy name," ver. 28. not in deliverance, but in instruction; for, for that he giveth thanks, " I will bless the Lord who hath given me counsel; my reins also instruct me in the night seasons," Psa. xvi. 7. His Father taught him and strengthened him, ver. 8—11. in his passion, and this was the hearing of his supplications. That is the best return of prayers which works our *good*, when not our *wills;* and when God doth not answer in the *letter*, if he answer in the *better*, we are no losers by our prayers : even devils themselves are heard to the letter, when his own Son is not: yet heard, in that he feared; and therefore when we have prayed, let us refer it unto God to determine the answer.

4. Hence we may learn how to judge of our afflictions, and of our deliverances from them

and it may serve instead of a use of examination: by this, I say, we may know, when our sufferings come in wrath, and when in love. You need not, as the scripture speaks in another case, say, Who shall ascend up into heaven, to look into God's book of life and death? or who shall descend into the deep of God's secret counsels, to make report hereof unto us? But what saith the scripture? "The word is nigh thee:" the word of resolution, to this inquiry, it is nigh thee, even in thy mouth, and in thy heart; that is to say, if thou canst evidence this to thine own soul, that instruction hath accompanied correction, that God hath taught thee as well as chastened thee, thou art a blessed man, thou shalt be saved: thou hast the word of him who is the author of blessedness, and *blessedness itself*, "Blessed is the man whom the Lord chasteneth, and teacheth him out of his law."

And therefore peruse, I beseech you, that model of Divine instructions or lessons, presented to you in the doctrinal part of this discourse, either at large, in those twenty particulars; or in the abridgement, the three great heads, to which they were reduced. And then, withal, set before your eyes those six properties of Divine covenant teaching, and compare your hearts and those lessons together. Ask your own souls, Hath God taught you those lessons, or any of them? 1. Inwardly. 2. Convincingly. 3. Experimentally. 4. Powerfully. 5. Sweetly. 6. Abidingly, (for even a hypocritical Ahab can humble himself for a time, walk in sackcloth, and go softly; a bulrush can hold down its head for a day.) And if the Spirit of God can bear witness to thy spirit, that thou art thus taught, happy art thou; bless the Lord, for the Lord hath blessed thee; thou mayst sing David's song, "I will bless the Lord who hath given me counsel; my reins also instruct me in the night season," Psa. xvi. 7. And again, "I know, O Lord, that thy judgments are right, and that thou in faithfulness hast afflicted me," Psa. cxix. 75. If I have been *less afflicted*, I had been *less blessed.*

But now on the other side, when there is no interpreter to accompany affliction, to expound unto man the meaning of the Almighty in his chastisements; when there is not a Divine sentence in the lips of correction; when the rod is dumb, or the creature deaf, and cannot hear the rod, and who hath appointed it; it is much to be feared, the stroke is not the stroke of God's children. O my brethren, it is sad when men come out of affliction the same they went in; when affliction leaves them as it found them; as ignorant, as unhumbled, as insensible of sin as sinfulness towards their suffering brethren, as worldly, as proud, as impatient, as unsavoury, as much strangers to Christ and their own hearts, as regardless of eternity: in a word, as fit for sin as they were before. This, I say, is exceedingly sad. And yet it is much sadder, when it may be said of a man, as once it was said of Ahaz; "In the time of his distress he did trespass yet more against the Lord," 2 Chron. xxviii. 22. It was an aggravation of wickedness, concerning which we may say, as our Saviour of the alabaster box poured on his head—Wherever the scripture shall be preached in the whole world, there shall also this which this man did be published; "*This is that king Ahaz.*" Surely it is a standing and a dreadful monument of reproach and infamy unto him to all generations. Christians, it is sad and dangerous beyond all expression when affliction serveth but as a gauge to give vent to the pride and murmur, the atheism and enmity, which is in men's spirits, against the Lord; when afflictions are but as oil unto the fire to irritate corruption, and make it blaze more fiercely; to continue in wonted sins, against such sensible and real proclamations to desist, is professed rebellion against God: a heavy indictment which the prophet bringeth against Jerusalem; " Thou hast stricken them, but they have not grieved; thou hast consumed them, but they have refused to receive correction: they have made their faces harder than a rock, they have refused to return," Jer. v. 3. In such cases it is to be feared, the cup of affliction is a vial of wrath, and the plagues of this life nothing else but some previous drops of that storm of fire and brimstone, wherein impenitent sinners shall be scorched and tormented for ever.

That scripture speaks dreadfully to this purpose, Jer. vi. 28—30. " They are all grievous revolters, walking with slanders; they are all corrupters; the bellows are burned, the lead is consumed of the fire; the founder melteth in vain; for the wicked are not plucked away; reprobate silver shall men call them, because the Lord hath rejected them." " They are all grievous revolters," that is, as the prophet Isaiah expounds it, " Ye revolt more and more," Isa. i. 5. Hebrew, They increase revolt, walking with slanders; they do not only revolt, but *slander* those that reprove their revolting; " They hate him that reproveth in the gate," Amos v. 10. they slander the prophets, and their words; nay, God himself doth not escape the lash of their tongues; they say, " The way of the Lord is not equal," Ezek. xviii. when they should condemn their own ways, they censure God's, " The way of the Lord is not equal." They are brass and iron. They would pass for silver and gold, a sincere and holy people, while they are a degenerate and hypocritical generation. " They are all corrupters," Jer. vi. 8. " They have deeply corrupted themselves," Hos. ix. 9. they have corrupted all their doings, Zeph. iii. 7. " they have corrupted the covenant of Levi," the worship, the ordinances, the truths of God, Mal. ii. 8. " The bellows are burned in the fire," that is, the lungs of the prophets, which have preached unto them in the name of the Lord, rising up early, and lifting up their voices like trumpets, to tell Israel their transgressions, and the house of Jacob their sins, and stretching forth their hands unto them all the day long, they are spent. " The lead is consumed," that is, all the melting judgments and chastisement, which, as lead is cast into the furnace to make it the hotter, God added to the ministry of the prophets, to make the word more operative, they will do no good. All this while, " the founder melteth in vain," whether God the master-founder, or the prophets, God's co-founders, or fellow-workmen, as the apostle calls them; they all melt in vain, 2 Cor. vi. 1. all their labour is lost; neither word, nor rod, neither judgments nor ordinances, can stir them; they refuse to receive correction, they will not be taught. Men will give God the hearing, but are resolved on their own courses. " The wicked are not plucked away." They are the same that ever they were; the swearer is a swearer still, and the drunkard is a drunkard still, and the unclean person is unclean still; " The vile person will speak villany, and his heart will work iniquity, to practise hypocrisy, and to utter error against the Lord," Isa. xxxii. 6. the unjust are unjust still, and the ignorant are ignorant still; nothing will better them, wicked they are, and wicked they will be. What follows? a formidable sentence; " Reprobate silver shall men call them." They would be counted silver, but it is reprobate silver, refuse silver, dross rather than pure metal; and their hypocrisy shall be made known to all men; " Reprobate silver shall men call them;" and happy they, if it were but the censure of mistaking men only; nay, but the Searcher of hearts hath no better thoughts of them; men do but call them so, because God called them so first; " Reprobate silver shall men call them, because the Lord hath rejected them." God hath cast them out as the founder casts out his dross to the dunghill, and they shall never stand among the vessels of honour, in whom the Lord will be glorified. A fearful sentence! the sum whereof is this—That when teaching goeth not along with correction, when men come out of the furnace, and lose nothing of their dross, it is a sad indication of a reprobate spirit, without timely and serious reflection, nigh unto cursing. " O consider this, you that forget God" and his chastisements, " lest he tear you in pieces, and there be none to deliver," Psa. l. 22.

5. A fifth branch of information may be to teach us thus much—That they may be blessed whom the world accounts miserable. The world judgeth merely by outward appearances, and therefore may easily be mistaken. They see the chastisement which is upon the flesh, and thence conclude a man miserable; but they cannot discover that Divine

teaching which is upon the spirit, which truly rendereth him incomparably blessed. The men of the world are incompetent judges of the estate and condition of God's children. The godly man's happiness or misery is not to be judged by the world's sense and feeling, but by his own; it lieth inward (save only so far as by the fruits it is discernible) and the world's faculty of judging is only outward, made up of sense and reason; therefore said the apostle, " The spiritual man judgeth all things, yet he himself is judged of no man;" that is, he is able to judge of the condition of the men of the world, but the men of the world are not able to judge of his condition, because it is above their faculty. The natural man *thinks* the spiritual man, under affliction, to be miserable; but the spiritual man *knows* the natural man, in the midst of his greatest abundance and bravery, to be miserable *indeed.* Therefore may the saints in their troubles think it, with St. Paul, a very small thing to be judged of man's judgment, 1 Cor. iv. 3. This is but man's day of judging; so the word signifieth; God's day is coming when things and persons shall be valued by another standard. Christ in his day shall judge not after the sight of the eyes, that is, not as things appear to sense and reason; nor after the hearing of the ears; that is, according to the report of the world; but with righteousness shall he judge; that is, he shall judge of things and persons as they are, and not as they appear. Moreover, this is also another comfort: " We have the mind of Christ," 1 Cor. ii. 16. the judgment of Christ, by virtue whereof we are enabled, in our measure, to judge of things and persons, as Christ himself judgeth.

6. A sixth branch of information—Is chastisement a blessing when accompanied with instruction? See then, and admire the wisdom, power, and goodness of God, who can make his people better by their sufferings. Who knows how to fetch oil out of the scorpion, to extract gold out of clay! to draw the richest wine out of gall and wormwood! that can turn the greatest evil of the body to the greatest good of the soul! the curse itself into a blessing! that can make the withered rod of affliction to bud, yea to bring forth the peaceable fruits of righteousness to them that are exercised thereby! Behold I show you a mystery: sin brought affliction *into* the world, and God makes affliction to carry sin *out* of the world. Persecution is but the pruning of Christ's vine, &c. The almond tree is said to be made fruitful by driving nails into it, letting out a noxious gum that hindereth the fruitfulness thereof. God never intendeth more good to his children than when he seems to deal most severely with them. The very heathen have observed it to us : God doth not love his children with a weak womanish affection, but with a strong masculine love, and had rather they suffer hardship than perish : " Whom the Lord loveth he chasteneth, and scourgeth *every* son whom he receiveth." God will rather fetch blood, than lose a soul; break Ephraim's bones, than suffer him to go on in the frowardness of his heart. Destroy the flesh, that the spirit may be saved in the day of the Lord Jesus. " We are chastened of the Lord, that we should not be condemned with the world," 1 Cor. xi. 32. His discipline is made up of severity and love ; he doth chastise, but he will teach also, that so his children may inherit the blessing ;

the discipline is sharp, but the end is sweet. " Bless the Lord, O my soul, and all that is within me bless his holy name : bless the Lord, O my soul, and forget not all his benefits."

7. It shows us, that a suffering condition is not so formidable a thing as flesh and blood doth represent it. It is ignorance and unbelief which slandereth the dispensations of God, and casteth reproach upon the cross of Christ. He that heard the words of God, which saw the vision of the Almighty, having his eyes opened, could by way of holy triumph ask this question, " Wherefore should I fear in the days of evil?" Psa. xlix. 5. which denotes, What is there in an afflicted estate so much to be dreaded? let any man show me a reason, and I will give way to fear and despondency. And that is more observable which follows; " When the iniquity of my heels shall compass me about?" This is an addition of the greatest weight and wonder imaginable; the meaning is—When my transgressions pursue me so close, that they even tread upon my heels, as it were ; when sin itself hath brought me into the snare, when God is correcting me for my iniquities; why truly, christians, that is the thing which a child of God doth most of all tremble at, to consider that he hath *sinned himself* into a suffering condition. In sufferings purely evangelical, namely, persecution for righteousness' sake, a gracious heart can see, many times, more cause of rejoicing than of perplexity, and look upon them as a gift rather than an imposition ; but afflictions and miseries, which sin brings upon a man, seem to be judicial and penal, and carry a face of wrath rather than of love. Observe it, even in these the psalmist can see no just cause of fear;

"Wherefore should I fear in the days of evil, when the iniquity of my heels shall compass me about?" See, when sin and sorrows besiege him on every side he is fearless, and knows no reason to the contrary, unless any one can tell him what it is: How so? surely upon the same account in my text, because David had a God that could teach as well as chastise; and therefore, though sin were as poison in his cup of affliction, yet Divine teaching could antidote that poison, and turn it into a cup of blessing unto him: " Thy rod and thy staff comfort me," Psa. xxiii. 4.

O that the children of God in affliction, or entering upon sufferings, would sit down and dwell upon this consideration, the fruit and advantage which God knoweth how to bring out of all their sorrows, even the peaceable fruits of righteousness. This would keep them from uncomely despondencies and dejections of spirit; " For this cause we faint not," saith the apostle, 2 Cor. iv. 16. 18. For what cause? " while we look not at the things which are seen, but at the things which are not seen ;" that is to say, not at the visible sufferings, but at the invisible fruit and advantage of our sufferings. This holds up head, and keeps up heart; and maketh the soul not only to be patient, but to glory in tribulation; " Knowing that tribulation worketh patience, and patience experience, and experience hope; and hope maketh not ashamed; because the love of God is shed abroad in our hearts by the Holy Ghost which is given to us," Rom. v. 3—5. This is the way to counterpoise the temptation; and in the conflict between the flesh and the spirit, to come in to the succour of the better part.

8. It shows us the reason why God doth keep

some of his people so long under the discipline of the rod.   Truly God doth not only bring his children into the school of affliction, but many times keeps them long there: " The rod of the wicked indeed shall not *always* rest on the back of the righteous," Psa. cxxv. 3.   But it may lie long, for months, for years, for many years together; seventy years were the Jews in the house of correction at Babylon; four hundred years in the brick-kilns of Egypt.   History and experience will serve in instances without number.   Hence you have the people of God so often at their *how-longs* in their sufferings, " But thou, O Lord, *how long?*" Psa. vi. 3.   " *How long* wilt thou forget me, O Lord? for ever? *How long* wilt thou hide thy face from me? *How long* shall I take counsel in my soul? *How long* shall mine enemy be exalted over me?" Psa. xiii. 1, 2.   In this psalm where my text is, " *How long* shall the wicked, *how long* shall the wicked triumph?" twice *how long*, before he can vent his complaint; and yet again the third time, " *How long* shall they utter and speak hard things?" " *How long*," cries Jeremiah, " shall I see the standard, and hear the sound of the trumpet?" Jer. iv. 21.   And Zechariah, " O Lord of hosts, *how long* wilt thou not have mercy on Jerusalem, and on the cities of Judah?" Zech. i. 12. The souls under the altar, Rev. vi. 10. cry with a loud voice, " *How long*, O Lord, holy and true, dost thou not avenge our blood on them that dwell on the earth?" Verily God doth keep his people, sometimes, so long under their pressures, that they begin at length even to give themselves up to despair, and to conclude they shall never see deliverance.   Thus you find not only the common multitude of the Jews in the Babylonian captivity, concluding desperately, " Our bones are dried, our hope is lost, we are cut off for our parts," dry bones may as well live, as our captivity have an end; but even the prophet Jeremiah himself, (whether in his own person, or in the name of the whole church, I know not, possibly both,) " They have cut off my life in the dungeon, and cast a stone upon me," Lam. iii. 53. He seems to himself to be in the condition of a man that is dead and buried, and the grave-stone rolled to the mouth of the sepulchre: a metaphor expressing a hopeless and desperate condition: yea hence it is, that when deliverance is nigh, they cannot believe it, though a prophet of God, or an angel from heaven, should report it. " Thou shalt arise, and have mercy upon Zion; for the time to favour her, yea the *set time* is come," sings the prophet Daniel, or some other that lived near the expiration of the seventy years' captivity; and yet in the mean time the Jews reply as before, " Our bones are dried, our hope is lost, we are cut off for our parts;" which means, Tell not us of God's arising, &c. we shall never see Zion again, we are but dead men. Observe it by the way, they that would not believe the captivity while it was in the *threatening*, Hab. i. 5. would not believe deliverance when it was in the *promise;* a just judgment upon them, that those who *would* not believe God threatening *should* not believe God promising. But that is not all; deliverance was so incredible after so long a captivity, that they could not believe it when they saw it. " When the Lord turned again the captivity of Zion, we were like them that dream," Psa. cxxvi. 1. They knew not, as it fared with Peter, half awake and half asleep, Acts xii. 9.

whether it was true, or whether they saw a vision only ; is this a real deliverance? or are we in a dream only? Our Saviour tells us, that when the Son of man shall come, (that is with particular deliverances to his church,) he shall not find faith on the earth, Luke xviii. 8. there will not be faith enough in the people of God to believe it, by reason of the long pressures and persecutions that have been upon them.

Now, I say, what is the reason that God suffers affliction to lie so long upon the backs of his children? Truly one reason is, because they have lived long in sin ; they have been long sinning, and therefore God is long correcting. God puts them to *their how-longs*, because they have put God to *his how-longs.* " *How long* refuse ye to keep my commandments, and my laws? *How long* will this people provoke me? and *how long* will it be ere they believe?" Exod. vi. 28. " *How long* shall thy vain thoughts lodge within thee?" Jer. iv. 14. " *How long* will it be ere they attain to innocency," &c. Hosea viii. 5. And truly if they have made God complain of *their how-longs*, no wonder if God make them complain of *his how-longs.* But then again, another and the main reason is, because the work is not yet done ; they do not receive instruction by their correction, else affliction would quickly cease. God giveth not a blow, he draws not a drop of blood, more than *needs ;* " For a season, if *need* be, ye are in heaviness," 1 Pet. i. 6. If there be *heaviness*, there is *need* of it ; and if heaviness *continue long*, there is *need* of it. It is not to gratify their enemies that God keeps them so long under their lash, but to teach them ; not that God afflicts willingly, &c. Lam. iii. 33. but that he may do them good in their latter end; that by the rod of correction he may drive out that folly which is in their hearts. And when that is done, then they shall stay no longer for their deliverance; then God opens the prison doors, and throws the rod into the fire; and infinite mercy it is, that they are *not delivered* till they are *bettered;* that God will not cease *chastening* till they are willing to cease *sinning;* saying, " I have borne affliction, I will offend no more ; that which I see not, teach thou me ; and if I have done wickedly, I will do so no more."

9. Take notice from hence, what unteachable creatures we are by nature, who will not set our hearts to receive instruction till we are whipped to it by the rod of correction, and hardly then. Unless God multiply stripes, it is not multiplying of precepts that will do us good ; there must be stripe upon stripe, and affliction upon affliction, as well as line upon line, and precept upon precept, or else it is in vain. We are so brutish, with Ephraim, that we make God spend his rods upon us ; and when all is done, God must turn us by main strength, or else our folly will not depart from us. This is a lamentation, and should be for a lamentation. We would say, that were a very bad child that will be taught no longer than the rod is upon his back! such are we ; we are so indocile that we put God to it, as it were, to study what methods and courses to take with us ; " How shall I do for the daughter of my people ? I will melt them, and try them," &c. Jer. ix. 7. Well, let us judge ourselves, and justify God.

10. It showeth us, on the contrary, how much gracious hearts are in love with the word, for the

improvement of their spiritual knowledge wherein, they can put such an estimate upon their sufferings; and account that their blessing which other men call their misery. " Blessed is the man whom thou chastenest and teachest." The psalmist in another place speaketh very warmly to this purpose; " It is good for me that I have been afflicted," Psa. cxix. 71. Why? that I might learn thy statutes. He loveth the word so dearly, that for the word's sake, he is in love with affliction. The whip, the rod, the prison, the wilderness, any thing, is precious that brings instruction with it. Carnal people can be content to die in their ignorance, so they may die in their nest; whereas gracious hearts think not much to go to school to a prison; and even while the blood is running down the back can say, It is good, because they are taught by it. O the different account that grace and nature make of the same dispensation! it is proud disdain to scorn to be taught by the lowest of God's ushers. The treasure is precious, though in an earthen vessel: there is none too old, none too wise, none too high, to be put into the meanest school on this side heaven.

I have done with the use of information: I come now, in the second place, to the

II. Use of exhortation.

And it is to four sorts of people: 1. Such as are yet free from sufferings; 2. Such as are under sufferings; 3. Such as are come out of a suffering condition; 4. Parents, in reference to their children.

1. The first branch of exhortation is to such as through the patience and forbearance of God are yet free from chastisement and affliction; the

candle of the Almighty doth shine in their taber-
nacle, and they wash their steps in butter, &c.
Why now, would ye prevent chastisement, and keep
off the strokes of Divine displeasure from yourselves
or families?   Let me commend unto you a twofold
caution from this doctrine :

(1.) Study these lessons well while ye are in the
school of the word.

(2.) Labour to be instructed by the chastisements
and afflictions which you see upon other men.

(1.) If you would prevent chastisement, study
these and the like lessons well, while ye are under
the teachings of the word. Therefore doth God
send us into the school of affliction, because we
have been non-proficients in the school of the
gospel : because we will not hear the word, we
force God to turn us over to a severer discipline,
and to have our ears bored with affliction ; and then
saith God, " Now hear the rod, and who hath appointed it."   O my beloved, labour, I beseech you,
to profit much by the teachings of Jesus Christ in
the gospel : set your hearts to all the truths and
counsels of God revealed to you therein. The
gospel is the model or platform of sound words,
able to make you sound christians, wise to salvation, 2 Tim. i. 13.   O let your profiting be made
known to all men.   In special, set your hearts to
those instructions or lessons propounded in the
doctrinal part of this subject ; for the neglect
whereof God is forced to send his people into captivity, that there he may teach them with the briers
and thorns of the wilderness.   In particular—

Learn, in the time of your peace and tranquillity,
to lay to heart the sufferings of the rest of your
brethren that are in the world.   " Remember them

that are in bonds, as bound with them," Heb. xiii.
3. Think of them that are in prison, whose feet
are hurt in the stocks, and the irons do enter into
their soul, with the very same affection and affliction of spirit, as if you yourselves lay bound in
chains by them in the same dungeon; put your
souls in their souls' steads : and content not yourselves with those loose, and fruitless, and transient
glances, which those that are at ease in Zion do
usually cast upon men in misery; a cold "Lord
have mercy on them," and there is an end. "Remember them that are in bonds, *as bound with
them;*" and that you may know you are not to
confine your compassion to prisoners only, it follows, "and them that suffer adversity," &c. Learn
to sympathize with all the people of God under any
adversity whatsoever ; hide not your eyes, and shut
not up your bowels of compassion from any that
are in a suffering condition ; and that upon this
account, "As being yourselves in the body." If the
duty respect thy brother, the motive respects thyself; thou are yet in the body: and while you
remain in the flesh, you cannot promise yourselves
one hour's exemption from troubles ; but are exposed to the same common calamities which attend
a state of mortality; as it is an argument of comfort to them that are in affliction, that their temptations and trials are common to men, 1 Cor. x. 13.
God doth not single them out to encounter with
unparalleled affliction: so on the other side it is an
incentive to compassion to them that are free, to
consider that they are liable to the same temptations ; and therefore should measure out the same
compassions to their suffering brethren, that they
would expect in the same trials ; not knowing how

soon the cup of trembling may be put into their own hand. Be sure, insensibleness of other men's miseries will hasten it: "They put far away the evil day; they lie upon beds of ivory, &c. eat lambs out of the flock, and calves out of the stall, &c. drink wine in bowls," &c. Amos vi. 3—6. that is, they give themselves up to all manner of sensuality and thereby drown the sense of their brethren's miseries; they are not grieved for the afflictions of Joseph: they lay not the affliction of the church to heart, it never cost them an hour's sleep, they abated nothing of all their sensual excesses; they never turn aside to shed one tear over bleeding Zion in secret: what follows; "Why," saith God, "therefore now shall they go captive with the first that go captive, and the banquet of them that stretched themselves shall be removed," ver. 7. As if God should have said; As I live, because you have not pitied your brethren in captivity, you your- selves shall be led away captive, and the next turn shall be yours; and there you shall learn by expe- rience, what it is to be plundered, and what it is to lie in chains, what it is to have cruel taskmasters set over you, what it is to want bread. You shall banquet it no more: you shall feel by sense what you would not feel by sympathy. And therefore, christians, set your hearts to the afflictions of the church and people of God; it is the great duty which the times call for; and I am afraid God is now visiting England and London for the neglect of this duty. We are verily guilty concerning our brethren, in Germany, in Ireland, in England, and Scotland, &c. in that we saw the anguish of their souls, when they besought us, and we would not hear; therefore is this distress come upon us. We have not grieved their sorrows, nor wept their tears, nor sighed their groans, nor bled their blood ; and therefore may fear, lest God should say unto us also, even unto us, " With the next that go into captivity, they shall go into captivity :" with the next that are plundered and spoiled, London shall be plundered and spoiled ; with the next that shall be imprisoned, you shall be taken prisoners ; with the next that shall be slain with the sword, you shall be slain with the sword ; your wives shall be made widows, and your children shall be made fatherless, and your dwellings shall cast you out, and be left desolate. And therefore let us look to it, and know in this our day the things of our peace, before they be hid from our eyes.   Show compassion, that you may not need compassion, or, if you need it, you may find it.

In like manner set your hearts to the other lessons which God teacheth by his chastisements.

Prize creature comforts more, and surfeit upon them less : be more thankful, and less sensual. Especially prize a gospel while ye have a gospel ; prize it by its worth, that you may not prize it by the want, Amos viii. 11. prize it that you may keep it, lest you prize it one day when you cannot recover it.   That is a dreadful word, " They shall go with their flocks and with their herds to seek the Lord, but they shall not find him," Hosea v. 6. " And I will send a famine, not a famine of bread, nor a thirst for water, but of hearing the words of the Lord," Amos viii. 11. " And they shall run to and fro, to seek the word of the Lord, and shall not find it," ver. 12.

Study self-denial, meekness of spirit ; labour to discover the hidden corruptions of your own hearts ;

be still digging into that dunghill, you will find it a bottomless pit. "The heart is deceitful above all things, and desperately wicked : who can know it? I the Lord search the heart," Jer. xvii. 9, 10. O, entreat the Lord to discover your hearts to you.

Study scripture evidence for your interest in Christ: rest not in any evidence, which you will not venture your souls upon, if you were to die this moment.

Labour to maintain sweet communion with God; to be able to say with the apostle, and to say truly, "Our fellowship is with the Father, and with his Son Jesus Christ," 1 John i. 3. Make God your choice, and not your necessity; and labour to maintain such constant converse with him, that when you die, you may change your place only, but not your company.

Live up in the exercise of your graces : "Add to your faith virtue, to virtue knowledge, and to knowledge temperance, and to temperance godliness, and to godliness brotherly kindness, and to brotherly kindness charity," 2 Pet. i. 5—7. Be adding one grace to another, and one degree of grace to another, and one exercise of grace to another exercise of grace, that you may not put God to add affliction to affliction, and sorrow to sorrow : while others are adding sin to sin, drunkenness to thirst, do you add grace to grace : "Be stedfast and unmovable, always abounding in the work of the Lord," &c.

Acquaint yourselves with God, and good shall come thereby, Job xxii. 21. Study to know God more, and love him better : "This is life eternal," &c. John xvii. 3. "Then shall we know, if we follow on to know the Lord," Hos. vi. 3.

Mind, I beseech you, while you are in your strength and peace, that one thing necessary : there is but one thing necessary ; there are many *may-be's*, but one *must-be.* O take heed of industrious folly, and dispirit not yourselves in the pursuit of trifles ; mind your work.

Redeem the time, the days are evil. O that christians would study the worth of time ; value a day : say of every hour, yea of every moment, This is time. Redeem time while you have it : redeem time while time may do you good. Evil days are coming, wherein you will say, I have no pleasure in them. Yea, the days are evil; evil with sin, evil with sorrow : redeem the time to do good, to receive good, that neither you may be the worse for the times, nor the times for you. Happy shall that man be called, who contributeth not to the heap of the God-provoking abominations, nor receiveth impressions from the hypocrisy and prevarication of the present generation !

Study the sufferings of Jesus Christ. Resolve, with Paul, to know nothing but Jesus Christ, and him crucified. A due contemplation of the cross will heighten Christ's love, and lessen your own sufferings.

And labour to get your conversation in heaven : looking for, and hasting to, or, as the word signifies, hasting, the coming of Christ, 2 Pet. iii. 12. Say, Come, Lord Jesus Christ, come quickly.

In a word, brethren, study, and study thoroughly, the sinfulness of sin, the emptiness of the creature, the fulness of Christ. And in all these, and the like lessons, labour for an inward, convincing, experimental, powerful, sweet, abiding teaching.

Content not yourselves, christians, with a gene

ral, slight, superficial, unsavoury, powerless, flitting knowledge. Rest not in notions; be not satisfied with expressions without impressions; nor with impressions, that are not abiding impressions, that are like figures written in the sand: this is the ruin of professors. Those professors, their names shall be written in the dust, who write Divine instructions in the dust: at least, if God have a mind to do you good, expect that he should send you into the house of correction, and there teach you with scourges, and write his instructions in your blood.

And therefore if you would prevent so severe a discipline, O improve your time well in the school of the word; "While you have the light, walk in the light, lest darkness come upon you," John xii. 36. While you sit under the teachings of the gospel, labour to get knowledge answerable to the means, and grace answerable to your knowledge. Thus much for the first caution.

(2.) If you would prevent affliction, labour to be instructed by the chastisements which you see upon other men. God deals with his children as tutors do with the children of princes, whip them upon strangers' backs. Thus God scourged Israel upon the back of the nations round about: "I have cut off the nations, their towers are desolate, I made their streets waste that none passeth by, their cities are destroyed, so that there is no man, that there is none inhabitant," Zeph. iii. 6. Short work! but their punishment was Israel's caution; "I said, Surely thou wilt fear me, thou wilt receive instruction." The world's judgments are the church's instructions, and God looked that his people should have made that use of this practical doctrine; " I said, Surely thou wilt fear me, thou wilt receive instructions." God had gracious ends in this dispensation ; his severity to strangers was his tender mercy towards Israel ; he spared not the nations, that he might spare them, so their dwellings should not be cut off, ver. 7. God cut off the nations, ver. 6. that he might not cut off Israel. Behold (as the apostle saith in another case, Rom. xi. 22.) the goodness and severity of God ; severity to the nations, but goodness towards Israel if they had continued in his goodness, and received instruction by their neighbour's destruction. And as God punished Israel upon the nations' backs, so God punished Judah upon Israel's back ; " Go ye now to my place in Shiloh, and see what I did to it, for the wickedness of my people Israel," Jer. vii. 12. Israel's chastisements should have been Jerusalem's teachings, and by their stripes she should have been healed ; for the neglect whereof God is highly displeased, and speaks concerning this in a very angry dialect; " And I saw when for all the causes whereby backsliding Israel had committed adultery, I had put her away, and given her a bill of divorce ; yet her treacherous sister Judah feared not, but went and played the harlot also," Jer. iii. 8. God took it ill, that Jerusalem should slight the kindness of such a caution, and despise the counsel which was written to her in her sister's blood, which denotes—I would have made Jerusalem wise by Samaria's harms, and taught her by a rod which she only saw; but she feared not; she hardened her heart through unbelief, and either would not understand the caution, or dared me to my face to do my worst, while by her shameless whoredoms she went on to provoke me to jealousy. This hasteneth that judgment upon herself which she despised on others: Judah must feel Israel's rod, because she would not hear it. As Israel must suffer those judgments on the nations which she would not improve; by those very nations by whom she would not be instructed, she must be destroyed, Zeph. iii. 8. So Judah must feel what she feared not at a distance; she that would not tremble at her sister's divorce must suffer divorce herself, and be judged as women that break wedlock, &c. Ezek. xvi. 38. " And bear her own shame for her sins that she had committed more abominable than they," ver. 52.

Beloved christians, if we would prevent the like severity, let us take heed of the like security. God hath been a long time scourging England upon Germany's back, and upon Ireland's back, and upon Scotland's back; God hath for these many years scourged London on the back of all the cities and counties round about; and God doth daily scourge every one of us in particular upon the back of our suffering brethren, in divers kinds: his design is, that we should fear him, that we should receive instruction. If we altogether fail his expectation, we may fear that the same rods are preparing for our backs wherewith they have bled, yea that their rods shall be turned into scorpions to us, we sin worse than others, when we sin those very sins for which others have been punished before our faces, and add contempt to their transgressions; and how just will it be with God, if as we aggravate their sins, so he aggravate upon us their plagues; that we that would not be bettered by God's warning pieces, should be destroyed by God's murdering pieces; that we that would not see and learn, should feel and perish. Even particular judgments should be our documents; "Remember Lot's wife;" her pillar of salt should season our hearts, that when the judgments of God are abroad in the earth, we that are the inhabitants, not of the earth only, but of Zion also, may learn righteousness. Even those judgments which the magistrate doth execute by God's appointment, are chiefly for caution to standers by, that others may "hear and fear, and do no more any such wickedness," &c. Deut. xiii. 11. How much more those judgments which the Lord himself doth execute! See Psa. lxiv. 7—9. 2 Pet. ii. 6. When the father is correcting one child, the whole family should fear and tremble. "Go to my place in Shiloh," saith God to the Jews, "and see what I did to it for the wickedness of my people Israel," Jer. vii. 12. If we would learn by other men's sufferings, we should prevent our own; this is the way to prevent sufferings.

The Lord make us wise to salvation.

2. I come to the second branch of exhortation. To such as yet lie under affliction, and the chastisements of the Almighty.

Take notice, O thou afflicted soul, what God's design is in afflicting thee, and make it thy design, namely, that thou mayst be taught, that correction may be turned into instruction; "Hear the rod, and who hath appointed it." It is the great mistake and folly of men, that they make more haste to get their afflictions removed than sanctified. "The captive exile hasteneth that he may be loosed, and that he should not die in the pit," &c. Isa. li. 14. which denotes that men would fain break prison, or leap out at the window, before God open the door; but this their

way is their folly; so the following words imply:
" But I am the Lord thy God that divided the sea,
whose waves roared; the Lord of hosts is his
name," ver. 15. which means, Men would fain
be delivered, but they take not the right course:
deliverance belongs unto me, " I am the Lord thy
God that divided the sea," and made it a way for
my ransomed to pass over, and that when it was
most tempestuous, when the waves thereof roared.
When I will deliver, no obstruction can stand in
the way; and yet Israel now in captivity will not
look to me: I am the Lord of hosts, that have all
the armies in heaven and earth at my command;
and yet when they are besieged with troubles and
dangers, I cannot hear from them, they run to the
creature and neglect God; or if they cry to me in
their distresses, it is for deliverance only, but not for
teaching, though " I have put my words in thy
mouth," ver. 16. that is, I have given them my laws
and statutes, wherein I have made known my
design in affliction, why I send them into captivity,
namely, that there I might *teach them;* that I
might humble them, and prove them, and make
them know what is in their heart. This is the
shortest way to deliverance, and in this path if they
had trod, " I would have planted the heavens, and
laid the foundations of the earth," ver. 16. even the
new heavens and the new earth of Jerusalem's
restoration, and have said to Zion, " Thou art my
people," in the same verse. This is God's method
wherein he will own his people, and wherein if
they meet him, they shall not stay long for their
deliverance.

And therefore be wise, " O thou afflicted, tossed
with tempest, and not comforted," Isa. liv. 11. be

instructed, lest God's soul depart from thee; make more haste to be taught, than to be delivered; and choose rather to have thy affliction sanctified than removed. That is observable in Elihu's speech, Job xxxvi. 13. " Hypocrites in heart heap up wrath," that is, add to their own calamities ; why ? " They cry not when he bindeth them," Why as it is, Job xxxiv. 32. " That which I see not teach thou me : if I have done iniquity, I will do no more."

(1.) Consider, that this is God's design, that he might teach thee by his chastisements, and if thou crossest God's design, it is just with God to cross thy design ; if thou wilt not let God have his end in instruction, he will not let thee have thy end in enlargement. The only way to retard deliverance, is to make too much haste to be delivered; and he that believeth will not make haste.

(2.) Consider, that bare deliverance is not the blessing. I told you before, that deliverance alone is but the fruit of common bounty ; I will tell you more now : deliverance alone may be the fruit of the curse ; a man may be delivered in wrath, and not in love ; deliverance from one affliction may but make way for another, for a greater. Affliction may return, like the unclean spirit, with seven more worse than itself. So God threatens an unteachable people ; " If by these things ye will not be reformed, but will walk contrary to me," cross my design in my chastisements, " then will I walk contrary to you." I will cross your design, and instead of deliverance, " I will punish you yet seven times for your sins," Lev. xxvi. 23, 24. The blessing of correction is instruction: O let not God go till he bless thee. It is a sad thing to have *affliction*, but not the *blessing* of affliction ; to feel the *wood* of the cross, but not the *good* of the cross ; to taste the *bitter root*, but not the *sweet fruit* of a suffering condition ; the *curse*, but not the *cordial.* Truly in such a case one affliction may not only make way for another, for more, for greater ; but affliction here may make way for damnation hereafter ; and as one saith, By all the fire of affliction in this world, a man may be but parboiled for hell. And therefore mind instruction, study the lessons of a suffering condition, and be importunate for nothing so much as to be taught of God ; and to be taught not with a common teaching, but that special, covenant, saving teaching, which changeth the soul into the nature of the truth, and makes the soul holy as it is holy, and pure as it is pure, and heavenly as it is heavenly. He chastens us "for our profit, that we might be partakers of his holiness," Heb. xii. 10.

3. The third branch of exhortation is, to them that are come out of affliction and fiery trials. Sit down, christian, and reflect upon thyself, turn in upon thine own heart, examine thyself—Have teachings accompanied chastisements? hath the rod budded? cast up thy accounts. What hast thou learned in the school of affliction? not to go over the larger catechism of those twenty lessons again. View the abbreviate ; hath God discovered to thee the sinfulness of sin, the emptiness of the creature, the fulness of Christ? Is no evil like to the evil of sin? no good like to Jesus Christ? Is the world become an empty vanity, a mockery, a nothing in thine eyes? Canst thou say, " It is good I have been afflicted?" and canst thou point out that good, and say, Thus I had, this I have got by my sufferings ;

N 3

I know Divine truth more inwardly, more clearly, more experimentally, more powerfully, more sweetly than ever; it hath a more abiding impression upon my heart? I would speak a word,

(1.) To them that can evidence these teachings to their own souls.

(2.) To them that cannot.

(1) To those who through grace do find the fruit of affliction in the savory and saving teachings of God upon their hearts; let me by way of exhortation commend a threefold duty to you.

[1.] Study to be thankful.

[2.] Labour to preserve the teachings of God upon thy spirit.

[3.] Learn to pray for them that are afflicted, and what to pray.

[1.] Study to be thankful. Hath God taught thee as well as chastised thee? O say with David, " What shall I render to the Lord?" For consider how great things God hath done for thy soul.

God hath done more for thee, than if he had never brought thee into affliction and trouble, or than if he had brought thee out the same day on which he sent thee in: if he had delivered thee upon the first prayer that ever thou madest in thine affliction, it had not been a comparable mercy to his teachings of thee by affliction. Prevention and deliverance may be in wrath, but God never teacheth the soul but it is in love.

God hath doubled his mercy and loving kindness to thee, he hath commanded deliverance and instruction too: a twisted mercy; yea, as deliverance and instruction were the return of prayer, a treble, a multiplied mercy: which should greatly endear the heart to God, and make it sing with David, "I will love the Lord, because he hath heard the voice of my supplication," Psa. cxvi. 1. Upon the return of prayer in a single deliverance, God expects the return of praise, " Call upon me in the day of trouble, I will deliver thee, and thou shalt glorify me," Psa. l. 15. how much more when he wreaths and twists his mercies one in another! double, and treble, and multiplied mercy, calls for double, and treble, and multiplied thankfulness. When God loads us with mercy we should load him with our praises.

Instruction is the seal of God, which set upon correction doth seal up adoption and son-ship, to them that are exercised thereby; the children of affliction are, by Divine teaching, sealed up the children of promise: " If his children forsake my law," speaking of Christ's spiritual seed, " I will visit their transgression with a rod, &c. but my loving-kindness will I not take away," Psa. lxxxix. 31—33. I will visit them with the rod, that is, I will teach them with the rod, it shall be a rod of instruction to them, that is the children's portion; " If his children forsake me," &c. Heb. xii. 7. God deals with you as with sons. Behold, O thou christian soul, God hath done that for thee in thy sufferings, which possibly he denied thee in thy prosperity, given thee an evidence of thy son-ship; he hath made thy suffering time thy sealing time; and hath allured thee, and brought thee into the wilderness, and there hath spoken comfortably to thy heart," Hos. ii. 14. Thy Patmos hath been thy paradise wherein he hath given thee his loves.

God hath consecrated thy sufferings by his teachings: afflictions have taken orders, as it were, and stand no longer in the rank of ordinary providences, but serve now in the order of gospel-ordinances, officiating in the holy garment of Divine promises, and to the same uses. What is the great end and design of the promises? the apsotle tells us, "There are given to us exceeding great and precious promises, that by them we should be partakers of the Divine nature," 2 Pet. i. 4. that is, of gracious dispositions and qualities, which make the soul resemble God, holy as he is holy, &c. this is the end of Divine promises and ordinances; and mark, what the apostle Peter affirms of the promises, the very same doth the apostle Paul affirm of God's chastisements, " He for our profit, that we might be partakers of his holiness," Heb. xii. 10. See, by virtue of Divine teaching afflictions advanced to the same degree and office with gospel ordinances and promises; so that what hinders, why we may not give those titles of honour to afflictions, which the apostle here gives to the promises, and say, There are given unto us exceeding great and precious afflictions, that by them we might be partakers of the Divine nature, that is, made partakers of his holiness, Phil. i. 29. See, O thou afflicted soul, by teaching God hath changed the very nature of affliction; he hath turned thy water into wine; a prison, a bed of sickness, into a school, into a temple, wherein he hath taught thee into his own likeness.

As God hath consecrated thy sufferings, so he hath consecrated thee also by thy sufferings. As it is said of Christ, " He made the Captain of our salvation perfect through sufferings," Heb. ii. 10. as the Greek means, he consummated, or perfected; Christ became a perfect Mediator by his passion; the cross was the complement and absolution of his mediatorial office: hence you hear him cry upon the cross, "It is finished," John xix. 30. And thus also may it be said of the members of Christ; they are perfected by sufferings. Chastisement being coupled with teaching, is the consecration and consummation of the saints : "I fill up," saith Paul, "that which is behind of the afflictions of Christ in my flesh," Col. i. 24. the after sufferings of Christ. As Christ as a Mediator, so Christ as one body, with his members, is completed by sufferings : "I fill up that which is behind :" Christ is not full till all his members have had their measure of sufferings : you have need of patience, that when you have done the will of God, you may inherit the promises, Heb. x. 36. When we have done God's will, all is not done; there is somewhat to be suffered, without which the christian is not in a capacity to receive his inheritance ; you have need of patience, to carry you through the suffering part of your work, as well as the doing, that so being perfect, you may inherit the promises.

By adding instruction to correction, God hath crowned thee with the blessing: " Blessed is the man whom thou chastenest and teachest." God hath turned the crown of thorns into a crown of gold, and set it on thy head, and now brings thee forth wearing this crown, and shows thee, as it were, to the world as a monument of free grace, proclaiming before thee, " Thus shall it be done to the man whom God will honour."

Well then, christian, sit down, and consult with thine own soul, what to render for so rich a mercy; and behold, it is resolved to thy hand : " I will deliver thee, and thou shalt glorify me," Psa. l. 15.

Behold God hath not only delivered, but taught thee, now therefore he expecteth glory from thee.

Glorify God with *thy lips;* "I cried to him with my lips, and he was glorified with my tongue." Let the lips of prayer be turned into the tongue of praise ; make your tongues your glory, by proclaiming God's glory ; be telling what great things God hath done for you ; say with David, " Come and hear all ye that fear God, and I will tell you what he hath done for my soul," Psa. lxvi. 16. abundantly utter the memory of his great goodness, make his praise glorious.   Extol him in psalms of thanksgiving : " Sing unto the Lord, O ye saints of his, give thanks at the remembrance of his holiness," Psa. xxx. 4.   " He that offereth me praise, glorifieth me," Psa. l. 23.

Glorify God with *thy life,* live his praise ; hath God taught thee?   If thou wouldst glorify God, go and put all the lessons which thou hast learned into print ; " Show forth the praises of him that hath called thee out of darkness into his marvellous light," 1 Pet. ii. 9. print them in such a legible character, that whoso runs may read : *lip praise* is good, but *life praise* is better ; " He that offers me praise glorifieth me, and to him that ordereth his conversation aright will I show the salvation of God," Psa. l. 23.   It is good to speak so, that men may see ; that standers-by may be God's witnesses and yours, that you are taught of God ; and say, Lo, what hath God wrought! how holily, and humbly, and fruitfully, and self-denyingly do these servants of God walk since they came out of tribulation!   Live so, that you may take off the scandal of the cross of Christ, and bring men into love with a suffering condition : " Let your light so shine before men, that they may see your good works, and glorify your Father which is in heaven," Matt. v. 16. that you may be a little heaven sparkling with bright stars of Divine graces, as it was said of Joseph.

Now God hath taught thee, be thou ready to teach others. It is a debt which thou owest to all thou conversest with; when thou art converted, strengthen thy brethren. Communicate what God hath taught thee to thy yoke-fellow, children, servants, friends, upon all seasonable opportunities. Sanctified knowledge is communicative; freely thou hast received, freely give. God never lighted this candle, that it should be put under the bed, or under the bushel, Mark iv. 21. the bed of pleasure, or the bushel of profit ; but that it may be put into the candlestick of thy conversation, and so shine before men, that they may see, and glorify thy Father which is in heaven. This is indeed to glorify God.

[2.] Labour to preserve the teachings of God upon thy spirit. Study how to maintain that sweet gracious frame of heart into which God hath taught thee by affliction. It is the duty which christians should practise, as oft as they come from the word, or any other Divine ordinance. When we come out of a sabbath, we should sit down, and observe with what frame of spirit God sends us away from the ordinance ; if the ordinance hath left no savoury gracious impression upon the heart, to lie in the dust, and mourn, and commune with our own hearts, and lament after God. If there be an ordinance frame, we should rejoice in it, bless God for it, and labour to keep up such a frame upon the heart till the next solemn approach to God. Christians, how much more should this be our care and study when we come out of God's furnace, that solemn ordinance of affliction, to labour to maintain that melting frame of heart, that warmth and heat, that life and vigour which we have brought with us out of affliction. Look to yourselves, that ye lose not those things which God hath wrought in you, 2 John 8. To that end take a few means or helps.

First. Be often reading over the lessons which God hath taught you; frequently revive the remembrance of them in your heads, and work the impressions of them upon your hearts: labour not only to say them without book, but indeed to get them by heart. I tell you, christians, you have need to take much pains with yourselves, to keep the teachings of God alive upon your spirits. For be sure of this, that you will find a great difference between your hearts yet under affliction, and when the affliction is taken off; and without infinite watchfulness your hearts will be too hard for you: "The heart is deceitful above all things, and desperately wicked," Jer. xvii. 9. There is much of a Pharaoh-like disposition in every man, very prone to harden when the storm is over. It is sad and wonderful to consider, how a corruption will lie as if it were quite dead, while danger and death are before us, and how suddenly and powerfully it will revive; and without special take-heed, betray the soul, when the danger is over. That caution which God by Moses gave the Israelites in the wilderness, may make every wise christian to tremble: " I know their imaginations, which they go about, even now, before I have brought them into the land, which

I sware," Deut. xxxi. 21. Their hearts were secretly projecting for their lusts, even while they were yet smarting under the rod: and in the howling wilderness they are forecasting how to satisfy sense, and serve their carnal interests, when they should come into the land that flowed with milk and honey. Possibly, these were not downright resolves; but said the Lord, " I know their imaginations." O my brethren, we should hearken to the whisperings of lust in our own bosoms, and labour to suppress them; to crush the serpent while it is in the shell; for if there be such floatings of sin in the imagination, while yet in durance, what projecting and contrivements will there be in the heart when liberty and enlargement shall present temptations and opportunities? And therefore " keep we our hearts with all diligence," Prov. iv. 23. or as the Hebrew phraseth it, Of all keepings keep our hearts, for out of them come the issues of life: and when the days of affliction and trouble are gone, work truths, and counsels received, frequently and fixedly upon your consciences; that you may, like good scribes, instructed to the kingdom of God, bring out of your treasures things new and old, Matt. xiii. 52. and have always in a readiness wherewith to oppose and check temptation, and may practise every lesson which God hath taught you, in the season thereof.

Secondly. Renew, also, often upon your souls, the remembrance of the sharpness and bitterness of the affliction : it will be a notable corrective to sensuality, and give check to sinful excesses. The flesh will quickly grow wanton when it findeth ease; Jeshurun, when the neck was got from under the yoke, quickly " waxed fat, and kicked," Deut. xxxii. 15.

"They soon forgat his works, they waited not for his counsel, but lusted exceedingly," Psa. cvi. 13, 15. Works and counsel, chastisements and teachings were quickly forgotten, when once the affliction was over. They quickly forgot a barren wilderness, in a land that flowed with milk and honey. "They waited not for his counsel:" they grew weary of counsel, when once free from correction ; and chose rather to walk by the dictate of their own lusts, than of God's laws, till at length God grew as weary (if I may so say) of counselling, as they were of being counselled ; and "gave them up to their own hearts' lusts, to walk in their own counsels," Psa. lxxxi. 12. That they who would not live by God's counsels, should perish by their own. And therefore, you that are come out of the house of bondage, remember the sorrows of a suffering condition ; set not your heart so much upon the pleasure of your present enlargement, as upon the bitterness of your former captivity. The church found great advantage in it, when returned from Babylon : " Remembering mine affliction and my misery, the wormwood and the gall, my soul hath them continually in remembrance :" and what was the fruit of it ? it follows, " and is humbled in me," Lam. iii. 19, 20. The meaning is this ; The people of God among the Jews, that desired to keep close to God after their great deliverance, experienced a serious and constant remembrance of those seventy years' sufferings, to be an excellent preservative to that humble and gracious frame of heart, which God wrought them into, in their captivity. And yet that is not all ; as remembrance of affliction preserved humility, so humility strengthened faith : " This I recall to mind, therefore have I hope :"

tribulation wrought patience, and patience experience, and experience hope, &c. Rom. v. 3. By
the kindly operation of the remembrance of former
dispensations, she began to conceive good hope
through grace, that God had not chastened her in
wrath, but in love ; and that all her tribulations
were the fruit of the promise, not of the threatening ; a blessing, not a curse. Go you, and do likewise.

Third. Call often to mind the sad discourses
and reasonings, the fears and tremblings, which
you have had in your bosoms in the times of trouble
and distress. Thus the church, " I forgat prosperity," Lam. iii. 17. She had been so long in a suffering condition, that now she can scarcely remember
that ever she saw a good day in all her life : and at
length she sits down, and gives herself up to despair ; "And *I said*, My strength and my hope is
perished from the Lord." She remembereth what
unbelieving conclusions she made in her affliction ;
"*I said*," &c. And so the prophet Jeremiah, ver. 54.
" Waters flowed over mine head ; then *I said*, I
am cut off:" when he began to sink in the mire, he
remembereth how his heart began to sink with
fear ; he calleth to mind, what faithless language
his heart spake ; " *I said*, I am cut off."

Thus David, " *I said* in my passion," &c. Psa.
xxxi. 22. and cxvi. 11. and " Then *I said*, I am cast
out of thy sight," Jonah ii. 4. Hezekiah makes
a large narrative of what discourses he had in his
own soul, what time he had received the sentence
of death ; and leaveth it in writing to all posterity,
" The *writing* of Hezekiah king of Judah, when
he had been sick ; *I said* in the cutting off of my
days," Isa. xxxviii. 9, 10. what did he say ? truly

he uttered very strange complaints for such an
eminent saint as he was: " I shall go to the gates
of the grave; I am deprived of the residue of my
years: I shall behold man no more with the inhabitants of the world ; mine age is departed :" and
a great deal more to that purpose. The sum
whereof is this; I shall die, I shall die; I must
take my leave of this world, and worms must eat
my flesh in the grave, &c. Such uncomely words
he uttered ; but he remembereth them afterward,
and is contented to shame himself for them to all
the world : he puts his fleshly complaints in writing,
that he may humble himself, and caution, yea and
comfort others.

And thus, christians, should we do ; we should
call to mind our *saids ;* that is, we should sit down
and recount the impatiences and short-spirited-
nesses, the murmur and unbelief, the love of a
present world, the fear of death, the hard thoughts
of God ; all the irregularities and distempers of our
own spirits, in the time of tribulation ; " *I said, I
said,*" &c. Doubtless it would be of singular use,
as, to humble our souls, and to check corruption ;
so to endear and preserve the teachings of God
upon your souls ; while you might tune David's
thanksgiving, conceived upon some such like occasion, " Good and upright is the Lord : therefore
will he teach sinners in the way," Psa. xxv. 8.
which means, I sinned against the Lord in my
affliction, by my impatience, unbelief, unhumbled-
ness, &c. yet he was pleased, not altogether to leave
me without the teachings of his Spirit ; not because
I was good, but because he was good ; not because
I pleased him, but because mercy pleased him :
not because I was upright before him, but because

he was upright, true and faithful to his own promise, hath he done it ; good and upright is the
Lord, and therefore he hath taught me, though I
was a sinner, in the way.

Fourth. Remember your vows. When God, by
the fire of affliction, showed you your folly, discovered to you the hidden corruption of your
hearts, and brought your ways and doings to remembrance, which were not good; you were
ashamed, yea, even confounded, and said, as it is
in Job, " Lord, wherein I have done wickedly, I
will do so no more." But take heed it be not so
with you, as it was with backsliding Israel, of whom
God thus complaineth ; " Of old time I have broken
thy yoke, and burst thy bands, and thou saidst,
I will not transgress," Jer. ii. 20. which means, I
brought thee, hundreds of years since, out of the
land of Egypt, out of the house of bondage, and
then thou madest me fair promises, I remember
the kindness of thy youth, the love of thine es-
pousals, ver. 2. Thou saidst, I will do so no
more. Lord, I will be covetous no more, and
idolatrous no more, adulterous no more ; I will
murmur no more, I will no more depart from thee,
thou art the guide of my youth. Good words,
had she been as good as her word : but O read
what followeth, and tremble ; " When upon every
high hill and under every green tree thou wanderest,
playing the harlot;" that is, no sooner her old
heart and her old temptations met, but presently
they fell into mutual embraces. And this is the
temper of our hearts, for all the world: we are
very good while we are in affliction, and promise
fair; but no sooner is the trial over, but we forget
God's teachings and our own vows, and return into

the same course and fashion of conversation as before. Now therefore, if you would preserve the teachings of God upon your spirits, sit down, remember your vows ; and, spreading them before the Lord, say with David, " I will pay thee my vows, which my lips have uttered, and my mouth hath spoken, when I was in trouble," Psa. lxvi. 13, 14. Lord, through grace assisting, I will be as ready to pay my vows, now I am well, as I was to make vows when I was sick, &c. " Thy vows are upon me, I will render praises unto thee," Psa. lvi. 12. When you have made good vows, be as careful to make good your vows unto the Lord : " Vow, and pay unto the Lord your God," Psa. lxxvi. 11.

Fifth. If you would preserve the teaching of God upon thy heart, attend constantly and conscionably upon the ministry of the word. The truth is, the word and the rod teach the same lessons. The rod many times is but the word's remembrancer : and therefore as the rod quickens the word, so the word back again will revive and sanctify the teachings of the rod. They mutually help to set one another with deeper impressions. And therefore hear wisdom, " watching daily at her gates, waiting at the posts of her doors," Prov. viii. 34. if thou wouldst be blessed. It will be of a twofold advantage. 1. It will help your memories : as the rod repeateth the word, so the word will repeat the instructions of the rod ; the gospel will bring to remembrance what you have learned in the school of affliction. 2. It will quicken affection. To hear that repeated by the still sweet voice of the gospel, which before God taught you in the voice of thunder, this cannot but affect, and make you bespeak the gospel, as once the Israelites did Moses, " Speak thou unto us all that the Lord our God shall speak unto thee, and we will hear it, and do it," Deut. v. 25—27. but let us not hear the voice of God any more, that terrible voice of judgment, lest we die. And certainly God will take it as well at your hands as he did at Israel's, and will answer in some such language, I have heard the voice of this people, they have well said all that they have spoken: O that there were such a heart in them, that they would fear me and keep my commandments, that it might be well with them, ver. 28, 29. and that I might not bring upon them such evils as I have done, any more.

Sixth. Be often feeding that frame of heart which God hath taught thee into. Do by it, as thou daily beggest God would do by thee ; give it day by day its daily bread ; meditations suitable to the nature of that grace which thou wouldst maintain ; threatenings, promises truths, scripture considerations, agreeable to the lesson. Take heed of feeding corruption with thoughts of the sweetness that is in sin; take heed of starving grace by withdrawing from it suitable aliment. You will require at the nurse's hands the blood of your infants that are starved. Will not God be much more jealous over the births and issues of his own Spirit? meditate much upon the sinfulness of sin, the emptiness of the creature, the fulness of Christ, the exquisiteness of his sufferings, the severity of the last judgment, the torments of hell, the joys of heaven, the infinite perfections of the Divine nature, and the horror of eternity. Rich in meditation, and rich in grace.

Seventh. Be much in prayer. As it was not enough for God to make the first creation, but he must uphold it by the word of his power, Heb. i. 3. or else it would quickly have returned into its first nothing; so it is with the second creation, Heb. xii. 3. Christ is the finisher as well as the author of grace. He that hath begun a good work in you, must perfect it, Phil. i. 6. Stability only comes from the unchangeable God; and therefore pray, that God would put of his unchangeableness upon you. Pray as Luther was wont to pray, Confirm, O Lord, in us what thou hast wrought, and perfect the work thou hast begun in us to thy glory, so be it; which he seems to have taken out of Psalm lxviii. 28. " Strengthen, O God, that which thou hast wrought in us." Pray that prayer which David prayed over that liberal frame of heart which God had formed in his people for the service of the temple. " O Lord God of Abraham, and Isaac, and Jacob our fathers, keep this for ever in the imagination of the thoughts of the heart of thy people, and prepare their heart unto thee," 1 Chron. xxix. 18. or stablish their heart. O be earnest with God for stability of heart, that thy goodness may not be as the morning cloud, and as the early dew, Hos. vi. 4. but that it may in some proportion resemble the Author of it, and be yesterday, and to-day, and for ever the same, Heb. xiii. 8.

In a word, by all these means and helps, and what other God hath sanctified for this gracious end, labour, christians, to be such *out* of your afflictions, as you promised God and yourselves to be when you were *in;* that neither God nor your own souls may have cause to repent of your sufferings; that the fruit of chastening may be repentance never to be repented of, that is, never to fall back again. Having in your troubles repented of your sins, take heed when you are delivered, that you repent not of your repentance; and he that doth not repent *of* his repentance now, shall never have cause to repent *for* his repentance hereafter.

And thus I have done with the second duty of those who through grace do find they have been taught by affliction.

I come now to the third duty.

[3.] Pray for the afflicted; and when you pray, say, Lord, teach them, as well as correct them, that they may be blessed. O pray thus for England; she hath been a long time sorely chastised of the Lord, and yet hath been all this while like a bullock unaccustomed to the yoke; O pray, " Turn us, Lord, and we shall be turned: thou art the Lord our God." Pray, that God would teach England in this day of her visitation the things of her peace before they be hid from her eyes, Luke xix. 42. O pray that we may be instructed, lest God's soul depart from us. If correction go not forth into instruction; if England be not at length reformed by all the judgments of God upon her, she hath seen her best days, and may expect to be made desolate, a land not inhabited, Jer. vi. 8. there is no balm for our pain, neither any physician that can heal our malady.

Pray thus for all your friends, who are or have been in the furnace of affliction; pray that they may come forth as gold purified seven times in the fire, that they may lose nothing there but their rust or dross. Pray, Lord, what they see not, teach them, and if they have done wickedly, let them do so no more. One great use which christians should make of reading the scripture, is to learn from thence the language of prayer. And, O, that the professors of this age would in this particular learn what to pray, and how to pray for their brethren in tribulation. O that they would censure less, and pray more, and instead of speaking one of another, speak more one to another, and one for another ; that was the good old way; " Then they that feared the Lord spake often one to another," Mal. iii. 16. But O the tender, praying, healing, restoring spirit is departed ; and if christians stir not up themselves to call it back again, it is a sad presage that God is departing too; and wo unto us when God departeth from us, Hos. ix. 12. We are like water spilt upon the ground, that cannot be gathered up again. We judge before we inquire, and reject before we admonish. Our brethren, upon vain surmises, are to us as heathens and publicans, before we have been to them as christians and fellow members. And this we think becometh us, and we take a kind of pride and contentment in it. But O to inform, to convince, to exhort, to pray, to put the bone in joint again if out ; this were done like the disciples of Christ ; to show ourselves christians indeed, professors not of the letter, but of the spirit, and would gain our brethren instead of blasting them. Consider what I say, and the Lord give you a right understanding in all things.

And, thus much for such as are come out of affliction, and find that it hath been through free grace a teaching affliction.

(2.) But now secondly, to such as cannot evidence to their own souls that chastening hath been accompanied with Divine teaching in any gospel proportion, or at least are not deeply sensible of the want of it ; here is a word of exhortation for them, suffer it I beseech you ; roll yourselves in the dust before the Lord ; smite upon your thigh, sigh with the breaking of your loins, and cry out with Ephraim, " Thou hast chastised me, and I was chastised, as a bullock unaccustomed to the yoke," Jer. xxxi. 18. I have felt the blows of God, but that is all ; I have received no more instruction by all my correction than a brute beast ; or if I had, I have quickly lost it ; it is fled " like a bird, from the birth, &c. Hos. ix. 11. Truly thou hast cause to sit down and even wish for thy affliction again. God had put himself into thy hands, as it were, and thou hast let him go without the blessing, the blessing of saving instruction. How mayst thou even wish, I say, O that I were in prison again, in my sick bed again, in banishment again, and so as to other things. However, humble thyself greatly before the Lord, and wrestle mightily for the after teachings of God upon thy heart ; pray, " Turn me Lord, and I shall be turned : for thou art the Lord my God ;" what affliction hath not done, Lord do thou ; set omnipotency on work, and it shall be done ; " turn me, and I *shall be* turned ;" that so thy soul may yet speak to the praise of free grace. " After that I was turned, I repented ; and after that I was instructed, I smote upon my thigh : I was ashamed, yea, even confounded, because I did bear the reproach of my youth," Jer. xxxi. 19. Urge the Lord, as Samson did after his victory; " Thou hast given this great deliverance into the hand of thy servant, and shall I now die for thirst, and fall into the hand of the uncircumcised ?" Judg. xv. 18.

Say thou, Lord, thou hast given thy servant this great deliverance from danger and death, and shall I now perish for want of teaching, and go down to hell among the uncircumcised? " Teach me thy way, O Lord, I will walk in thy truth: unite my heart to fear thy name," Psa. lxxxvi. 11. " Teach me to do thy will; for thou art my God: thy spirit is good ; lead me into the land of uprightness," Psa. cxliii. 10. In a word, desire the Lord that he would do all the work, and then take all the glory. Say, Lord, teach me as well as deliver me, and I shall be blessed.

4. The fourth and last branch of exhortation is to parents and governors; to exhort them in the education of their children to imitate God; and that in two things.

(1.) In affording their children due correction.

(2.) To correction to add instruction.

(1.) Afford your children due correction. It is the counsel of the Holy Ghost, " Chasten thy son while there is hope, and let not thy soul spare for his crying," Prov. xix. 18. Behold, God counselleth you that are parents, or instead of parents, to do with your children as he doth with his ; wisely to use the discipline of the rod, before vicious dispositions grow into habits, and folly be so deeply rooted, that the rod of correction will not drive it out, Prov. xxii. 15. Error and folly, saith one very well, are the knots of Satan, wherewith he ties children to the stake to be burnt in hell; and these knots are most easily cut betimes; or if you should make the child bleed in cutting them, let it not cause you to withdraw your hand ; for so it followeth, " Chasten thy son, &c. and let not thy soul spare for his crying." It is not only foolish, but cruel pity to forbear correction for a few childish tears, to suffer the child to howl in hell for sin, rather than to shed a few tears for the preventing of it. Foolish fathers and mothers call this love, but the Father of spirits calls it hatred; " He that spareth the rod, hateth his son," Prov. xiii. 24. Surely there is nothing so ill-spared, as that whereby the child is bettered, such sparing is hatred; and because you *hate* your children *in* not correcting them, they come afterward to hate you *by* not correcting them. But that is not all; the parent's lenity in this case makes way for God's severity. Pity to the flesh is cruelty to the soul; so the Hebrew may be rendered, Spare not to his destruction, or to cause him to die, that is, to occasion his destruction. The foolish indulgence of the parent may be, and often is the death of the child, eternal death. Parents spare their children in their folly to the destruction both of body and soul. And this may help us to expound that other parallel text, " Withhold not correction from the child : for if thou beatest him with the rod, he shall not die," Prov. xxiii. 13. The meaning may be, either that correction will not kill him; the rod will break no bones; so preventing and reproving at once the silly and sinful tenderness of fond parents, who think if they should correct their children, they would presently die of it; they are as afraid to use the rod, as if it were a sword. Abraham feared not so much to sacrifice his son, as such parents fear to chasten him. Nay, but saith the Holy Ghost, fear not correction, for behold, the strokes of the rod are not the strokes of death; it is but a rod it is not a serpent, take it into thy hand ; it may smart, it will not sting. To obviate the fear of parents in this case, God himself giveth them his word for it, "He shall not die." This, I say, may be the meaning, By correcting thy child thou shalt not murder him.   Or else, which I rather conceive, the words may be a motive drawn from the fruit of correction; "Withhold not correction from the child;" why? "He shall not die," that is, it may be, and, through Divine blessing accompanying it, is often a means to prevent death: it may prevent the first and second death, to which the child is exposed by the sinful indulgence of the parent.   The word used in this place, saith one, seems to note an immortality; so that "He shall not die," is all one as if the Holy Ghost had said, He shall live for ever; the rod on the flesh shall be a means to save the soul in the day of the Lord Jesus: "We are chastened, that we should not be condemned with the world," 1 Cor xi. 32.   Such smitings, as David saith in another case, "shall be a kindness," Psa. cxli. 5. and such rebukes are so far from breaking the head, that they shall be an excellent oil which shall cure and give life.   The very philosopher could say, Correction is a kind of physic or medicine.   Alas, our children are sick, and cruel is that mercy which will suffer them to die, yea eternally, rather than disgust their palates with a little bitter physic.   Apes and monkeys they be in the forms of men and women who thus hug their little ones to death; parricides rather than parents; of whom we may say, as sometime the Roman emperor said of Herod, when he heard that he had murdered his own son amongst the rest of the infants in Bethlehem, that so he might be sure (as he supposed) to destroy the King of the Jews, Surely it were better to be such people's swine than their sons.   O hateful indulgence.

merciless pity ! to lose a child for want of correction ! such parents throw both the rod and the child into the fire at once ; the rod into the fire of the chimney, and the child into the fire of hell. This is not done like God, for, " Whom the Lord loveth he chasteneth, and scourgeth every son whom he receiveth," Heb. xii. 6. And so doth every wisely loving parent ; " He that spareth the rod hateth his son, but he that loveth him chasteneth him betimes," Prov. xiii. 24. As moths are beaten out of a garment with a rod, so must vices out of children's hearts.

And for want of this disciplinary love, how have some children accused their parents, on their death-bed, yea at the gallows ! and how many do and will curse them in hell, in some such language as Cyprian supposeth : The treacherous fondness of our parents hath brought us into these torments, our fathers and mothers have been our murderers ; they that gave us our natural life, have deprived us of a better ; and they that would not correct us with the rod, have occasioned us now to be tormented with scorpions. O it would grieve the heart of the most unnatural parent in the world to hear the doleful complaints, and those hideous yellings of poor children in hell fire, whom their fondness hath sent thither. And O that they would listen to them, before they themselves come into that place of torment, and *there* find *no mercy*, because *here* they have showed their children *so much.* The child goeth to hell for his wickedness, and the parent many times for his mercy. Yea even in this life, how do many godly parents smart for their fondness, because they will not make their children smart for their folly. Eli and David would not so much as

rebuke their sons, and God gave them both great
rebukes in their sons. It is said of Eli, "His sons
made themselves vile, and he restrained them not,"
1 Sam. iii. 13. the Hebrew signifieth, He frowned not
upon them. Oh sad ! for want of a frown to destroy
a soul ! the soul of a child ! to smile a child to hell !
Consider of it ; I am much afraid this unchristian,
yea, unnatural indulgence of parents, is the fountain
of all that confusion, under which England at this
time reels and staggers like a drunken man : and
for this very sin, at least for this among others, yea,
and for this above others, God is visiting all the
families of the land, from the throne to the poorest
cottage.   Parents have laid the foundation of their
own sorrows, their children's ruin, and the desola-
tion of the nation, in the looseness and delicacy of
their education ; and yet are not sensible of it to
this day.   We have not corrected our children, and
therefore God is correcting us in our children. We
have not crossed them in their unlawful desires,*
and therefore God doth cross us in our righteous
desires.   We have walked (even in this point, exceedingly) contrary to God, and to his discipline ;
and therefore God is walking contrary to us, and is
punishing us seven times more for this iniquity.
And therefore, O that parents would at length
awaken themselves, to follow both the pattern and
precept of their heavenly Father ; who, as he correcteth whom he loveth, so he commands them to
correct, if they love their children.   "Withhold not
correction from the child ; for if thou correct him
with the rod, he shall not die." If if be needful that

---

* God makes our children our rods, because we have
withheld the rod from them. We gave them too much rest,
and therefore they give us none, Prov. xxix. 17. Lev. xxvi.

the rod draw blood, it is for their safety; it is as the physician deals with them to prevent a fever; a fever of boiling passions here, and of boiling fire and brimstone hereafter: it is to cure, not to kill; yea, thou killest, if thou dost not wound: and therefore again I say, withhold it not. Give the rod unto thy child, and he will one day give thee thanks for it. Yea, it is worth observation, that the same word in the original, which is translated withhold, signifieth also to forbid; meeting with another distemper in parents, who as they will not correct their children themselves, so also they forbid others to correct them, under whose tuition they put them. As if they were afraid their children would not have sin enough here, nor hell enough hereafter, they lay in caveats against the means which God hath sanctified for their reclaiming. What tears of blood are sufficient to bewail this folly? You that are godly-wise, and wisely-loving, take heed of it; and when you commit your children to others' hands, do not in the mean while hold their hands. If thou judgest them not wise, why dost thou choose them? if thou choose them, why dost thou not trust them? Well then, if the rod be in thine own hand, withhold it not; if in thy friend's hand, forbid it not. Certainly there is great need of this duty, which the Spirit of God doth frequently inculcate all along the Proverbs. I will conclude this branch of the exhortation with inverting the counsel of our Saviour in this particular sense; Be ye not merciful, that you may be the children of your heavenly Father, Matt. v. 44, 45. for "whom he loveth he correcteth, and scourgeth every son whom he receiveth." Go, thou, and do likewise; and this shall be your mercy and love to your children: "He that spareth the rod, hateth his son; but he that loveth him, chasteneth him betimes," Prov. xiii. 24.

(2) You that are parents, or instead of parents, if you would have your children happy, add instruction to correction. Imitate God in this part of paternal discipline also; let chastisement and instruction go together. It is that which the Holy Ghost urgeth upon you; "Bring them up in the nurture and admonition of the Lord," Eph. vi. 4. There are two words relating to both these parental duties; in the chastisement or correction; and it is added of the Lord: that is, either in the chastisement, wherewith the Lord exerciseth his children; or in the chastisement which the Lord commandeth earthly parents to exercise towards their children: this is the first duty, of which already. And then there is another word, which holdeth forth the end and design of parental correction, and that is, in the admonition and instruction of the Lord: that is, in counsels and instructions taken out of the word of God, or such as are approved of by God. The sum is this, that while we chasten the flesh, we should labour to inform and form the mind and spirit, by infusing right principles, pressing and urging upon their tender hearts counsel, reproof, and instruction, as the matter requireth. This is the duty of parents, to imitate God, to let instruction expound correction; and with a rod in the hand, and a word in the mouth, to train up their children to life eternal. A dumb rod is but a brutish discipline, and will certainly leave them more brutish than it found them. Chastisement without teaching may sooner break the bones than the heart; it may mortify the flesh, but not

corruption; extinguish nature, but never beget grace. "But the rod and *reproof* give wisdom," Prov. xxix. 15. Instruction added to correction, as it makes excellent christians, so it makes good children. There are parents that are severe enough to their children ; they spare for no blows : instead of breaking them of their wills, by a wise and moderate correction, they are ready to break their bones, and their necks too sometimes, in their moods and passions. But they never mind the other branches of paternal discipline, instruction and admonition : of such parents I suppose the apostle speaketh; "We have had fathers of our flesh, who corrected and chastened us after *their own pleasure,*" Heb. xii. 9, 10. He speaketh not of *all* parents; but his meaning is, There are such men and women in the world, who are most unlike to God; and in smiting their children rather please themselves than profit their children. He *for our profit,* but they after their own pleasure, to give vent to their passion, and satisfy their vindictive rage and fury : and when is that ? truly when the rod and reproof do not go together; it is an argument there is more passion than judgment, more lust than love, in such chastisements. Such parents do rather betray their own folly, than take a course to make their children wise. The rod and reproof give wisdom : neither alone will do it : the rod without reproof will harden the heart, and teach the children sooner to hate the parent, than to hate sin; and reproof without the rod will leave no impression. "Reproofs of instruction are the way of life," Prov. vi. 23 or corrections of instruction : a lesson set on with correction is best remembered. It is Divine truth that must be the instrument of working saving grace in the heart : " Sanctify them through thy truth, thy word is truth," John xvii. 17. It is the commendation of Timothy's mother, that from his very infancy she instructed him in the " scriptures, which were able to make him wise to salvation," 2 Tim. iii. 15. When there is a Divine sentence in the mouth of the rod, it brings wisdom and life with it.

And therefore, O that parents would imitate the Father of spirits in this blessed art of paternal discipline: join the word of instruction to the rod of correction ; teach as well as chastise : " Reprove, rebuke, exhort with all long suffering and doctrine," 2 Tim. iv. 2. It is true, it is enjoined Timothy as a pastoral duty ; but it is as true, that every parent is a king, a prophet, and a priest: a king to govern and chastise ; a prophet, to teach and instruct ; and a priest, to offer up spiritual sacrifice to God, prayer and praise with and for the family. O that every child might have cause to give their parents that commendation, which once Augustin gave his mother. My mother, saith he, made it her business to make God my Father, because she travailed with my everlasting salvation, with more tenderness and sorrow, than ever she did with my first birth. O that natural parents could bespeak the fruit of their loins, as St. Paul bespeaks his Galatians, " My little children, of whom I travail in birth again, until Christ be formed in you," Gal. iv. 19. that so they might rejoice in the second, more than ever they did in the first birth. Why, this is done by the word and the rod. " Correct thy son, and he shall give thee rest ; yea, he shall give delight unto thy soul," Prov. xxix. 17. Correct! how ? the 15th verse answers ; the rod and reproof give wisdom ; thus give your children correction, and they shall give you rest and delight. Though correction for the present do not give them rest, for no chastening for the present seemeth to be joyous, but grievous; yet it will make them give you rest; and though correction doth not delight them, yet it shall make them give delight to you. What greater delight than to see your children walking in the truth! 3 John 4. and to think thus with yourselves, (not as Cassiodor expresseth it, that so many sons, so many counsellors to the state, but) that, so many children God hath given you, so many children you have brought up for God, and so many heirs for the kingdom of heaven. Well; chastise and teach them out of the law of God, and thy children shall be blessed. Which that they may, indeed, take one short caution more; and that is—

Add prayer to instruction. As teaching should accompany chastisement, so prayer should accompany teaching. God need use only the rod and the word ; because the blessing is in his own hand, he can command a blessing. It is not so with us; as Paul may plant, and Apollos may water, but God must give the increase; so the Father may correct, the mother may instruct, both may do both, but God must give the blessing : and therefore christian parents, while they add instruction to correction, should add prayer to instruction. Means are ours, success is God's; and therefore let us put the rod into the hand of instruction, instruction into the hand of prayer, and *all* into the hand of God. I knew a worthy gracious lady living in the city, who would never use the rod but as with much pious instruction before, so after, would cause the child, if of capacity, or ever it stirred from the place, solemnly to kneel down and beg a blessing of God upon it. Go you and do likewise. Pray, and teach your children to pray, that God would so bless correction and instruction, that both may make you and your children blessed. Amen.